McGRATH

EMILY STEAD

CLASSIC FOOTBALL HEROES

McGRATH

FROM THE PLAYGROUND
TO THE PITCH

DINO

First published in the UK in 2025 by Dino Books,
an imprint of Bonnier Books UK,
5th Floor, HYLO, 105 Bunhill Row,
London, EC1Y 8LZ
www.bonnierbooks.co.uk

X @UFHbooks
www.heroesfootball.com
www.bonnierbooks.co.uk

Text © Studio Press 2025

1 3 5 7 9 10 8 6 4 2

All rights reserved. No part of this publication may be reproduced, stored in a retrieval system, or transmitted in any form or by any means, without the prior permission in writing of the publisher, nor be otherwise circulated in any form of binding or cover other than that in which it is published and without a similar condition including this condition being imposed on the subsequent purchaser.

Paperback ISBN: 978 1 78946 916 5
E-book ISBN: 978 1 78946 943 1

The authorised representative in the EEA is Bonnier Books UK (Ireland) Limited.
Registered office address: Floor 3, Block 3, Miesian Plaza
50–58 Baggot Street Lower,
Dublin 2, D02 Y754, Ireland.
Email: compliance@bonnierbooks.ie

The views in this book are the author's own and the copyright, trademarks and names are that of their respective owners and are not intended to suggest endorsement, agreement, affiliation or otherwise of any kind.

This book is unofficial and unauthorised and is not endorsed by or affiliated with Paul McGrath.

A CIP catalogue record for this book is available from the British Library

Typeset by IDSUK (Data Connection) Ltd
Printed and bound in Great Britain by Clays Ltd, Elcograf S.p.A

For those on a tricky path, keep heading in search of adventure.

CLASSIC FOOTBALL HEROES

Emily Stead has loved writing for children ever since she was a child herself! Working as a children's writer and editor, she has created books about some of football's biggest stars, teams and tournaments for many a season. She remains a passionate supporter of women's football and Leeds United.

Cover illustration by Dan Leydon
To learn more about Dan, visit danleydon.com
Or follow him on Instagram or X @danleydon

TABLE OF CONTENTS

ACKNOWLEDGEMENTS................................. 9
CHAPTER 1 – **GLORY, GLORY, MAN UNITED!**........... 11
CHAPTER 2 – **MEETING MAM**....................... 18
CHAPTER 3 – **THE GRASS OF GLENSILVA**............. 24
CHAPTER 4 – **PEARSE ROVERS**..................... 29
CHAPTER 5 – **DALKEY DAYS**....................... 34
CHAPTER 6 – **THE BLACK PEARL OF INCHICORE**....... 41
CHAPTER 7 – **MOVING TO MANCHESTER**.............. 46
CHAPTER 8 – **CHALK AND CHEESE**.................. 52
CHAPTER 9 – **THE BOY IN GREEN**.................. 57
CHAPTER 10 – **JACK'S LAD**....................... 63
CHAPTER 11 – **THE ROAD TO WEST GERMANY**......... 68
CHAPTER 12 – **AN EPIC EUROS**.................... 73
CHAPTER 13 – **AN UNEASY EXIT**................... 79

CHAPTER 14 – **THE VILLANS' VOTE** 85

CHAPTER 15 – **AN ITALIAN ADVENTURE** 91

CHAPTER 16 – **ALL ROADS LEAD TO ROME** 98

CHAPTER 17 – **DIFFICULT DAYS** 103

CHAPTER 18 – **PREPARING FOR BATTLE** 109

CHAPTER 19 – **WORLD CLASS** 116

CHAPTER 20 – **KNOCKED OUT** 122

CHAPTER 21 – **A THIRD TROPHY** 127

CHAPTER 22 – **DERBY DEBUT** 133

CHAPTER 23 – **END OF AN ERA** 139

McGRATH HONOURS 149

GREATEST MOMENTS 152

TEST YOUR KNOWLEDGE 156

PLAY LIKE YOUR HEROES 158

ACKNOWLEDGEMENTS

My first thank you is to Bonnier Books UK for adding me to their squad! Ultimate Football Heroes is a special series that has the power to inspire all readers and fans of the beautiful game.

To every teacher, bookseller and librarian who has helped get the books into the hands of readers special thanks are due. And of course, an extra-special mention goes to you, the readers and fans – without you there wouldn't be any Heroes.

More thanks go to my mum and dad, who raised a reader in a house full of books, and always cheered on my own (very modest!) sporting successes.

Finally, a huge round of applause for all the players, parents, coaches, clubs, media and those working behind the scenes who all share a love of the beautiful game.

CHAPTER 1

GLORY, GLORY, MAN UNITED!

18 May 1985, Wembley Stadium, London
FA Cup Final – Everton vs Manchester United

For football fans in the 1980s, FA Cup final day was like a second Christmas Day, and the players felt just as excited for their chance to grace the famous turf at Wembley Stadium. It was here where England had won the World Cup back in 1966, where a host of great European finals had been decided, and where history continued to be made each year when it hosted the final of the world's oldest cup competition, the FA Cup.

In 1985, two great clubs of the English First Division were set to battle it out in the final. Favourites Everton were fresh from winning both the league and a European trophy called the Cup Winners' Cup. They had brilliant players in most positions.

Their opponents, Manchester United, were desperate to win a trophy after slipping up in the league that season, eventually finishing fourth. Manager 'Big' Ron Atkinson had led the club to FA Cup glory two seasons ago but was now under pressure to deliver more silverware.

At the heart of the United defence, centre-back Paul McGrath was now in his third season at the club. Injuries had limited his playing time since Atkinson had brought him over from the League of Ireland, but the manager was staying patient – he knew he had unearthed a jewel in Paul. The young defender was strong and athletic, yet so calm and elegant when up against the most dangerous of strikers.

Atkinson's first FA Cup victory when managing United had come in 1983 against Brighton and

Hove Albion, when the Red Devils had needed a replay to beat the Seagulls. Back then, only one substitute was allowed, and Paul sadly hadn't been picked to play.

Since then, Paul had watched and learned from the superstars in the Manchester United squad and become a better player. Now, two years later, he was starting as their Number 5.

'Don't sit back. Go at them!' were Atkinson's instructions.

Everton midfielder Peter Reid had the same idea, and fired an early warning shot. He was unlucky to see his volley deflected onto the post by the studs of John Gidman.

Phew! Paul clenched his fists.

Half-time arrived with neither side able to find the net in the Wembley heat. It was all to play for.

Everton kept pushing, and with just under fifteen minutes remaining, Reid robbed Paul on the halfway line. Behind Paul, Kevin Moran was the last defender. The Everton man was clean through on goal, when Kevin made a crunching tackle.

'OFF! OFF! OFF!' chanted the blue half of Wembley.

'That's a foul by Moran,' said the TV commentator, 'but it was clumsy more than anything.'

So when the ref reached into his pocket and pulled out a straight red card, the Man United players were left stunned. No one had ever been sent off in an FA Cup final before!

'Oh! He's sent him off. He's sent Moran off!' the commentator gasped.

The ref signalled to Kevin to leave the field.

'You're not serious?' Kevin tried to protest his innocence.

Even Peter Reid didn't think it was a foul!

Paul screwed up his face. It was a soft sending-off for sure, but he blamed himself. If only he'd been more alert, Kevin wouldn't have had to dive in! Now they had just twelve minutes to find a goal with only ten men.

'Concentrate,' Paul told himself determinedly.

After that, Atkinson reshuffled his team, with Frank Stapleton dropping back into defence to partner Paul.

Atkinson's tactics worked, and Manchester United ended the ninety minutes strongly.

And so to extra time. Paul still had plenty left in the tank. Yes, his team were a man down, but unlike Everton, Manchester United hadn't just played a European final a few days earlier. Everton were sure to start tiring.

'Anything can happen.' Paul stayed positive.

In the first half of extra time, Everton found the ten men of Manchester United hard to break down. United, meanwhile, hadn't looked like scoring either. With ten minutes to go, all signs were pointing to a replay.

Then came a moment of genius. United's midfield star Mark Hughes received the ball in his own half with his back to goal, turned gracefully and flicked a pass with the outside of his boot to young Norman Whiteside on the right wing.

'Now go!' Mark screamed.

Norman surged forwards, with the Everton defender Pat van den Hauwe staying tight, waiting for his chance to steal the ball.

But instead of driving into the box for a better angle to shoot, Norman spotted a gap. The next moment, he sent an incredible shot sailing past the keeper and inside the far post.

The kid's only gone and done it! Paul couldn't believe how easy his best friend had made that shot look.

'It's there! Whiteside!' the commentators boomed.

Paul breathed a huge sigh of relief.

Now that the ten men of Manchester United had the lead, they felt unstoppable. Their passes were precise, the tackles were timed to perfection and there were no more mistakes.

Ten more minutes and the Cup will be ours! Paul told himself.

The fans in red didn't stop singing, urging their team over the line, until the final whistle blew at last. They had done it – Manchester United had won the FA Cup at Wembley!

With every ounce of energy spent, Paul's knees suddenly gave way beneath him. He sank to the turf, as tears of joy began to prick his eyes. He had just won his first big trophy in football, wearing the colours of the famous Manchester United! What were they going to make of this back home in Ireland?

What a journey he'd been on, likely a hundred times harder than anyone else on the pitch. From being raised in Dublin orphanages as a small boy to looking like he might never kick a ball again as a teenager, Paul McGrath had beaten all the odds on the path to reach this moment.

Weary legs climbed the thirty-nine steps to Wembley's Royal Box to collect their medals. Paul clutched his own medal tightly, only letting go to raise his arms, when captain Bryan Robson lifted the trophy laced with ribbons in red, white and black. FA Cup glory belonged to Manchester United! Paul felt blessed to have played his part.

A few days later, the club showed off the famous trophy on an open-top bus. Fans lined the streets, waving from windows and clinging to lampposts, while cheering for Norman and Kevin . . . and Paul! It felt incredible.

And that's when it began to sink in. *I've really made it,* Paul realised. *I'm a professional footballer.*

CHAPTER 2

MEETING MAM

Mr and Mrs Donnelly's house in Whitehall, Dublin, was the happiest home that Paul had ever known. There, he felt safe and loved. The foster couple had three children of their own, a son and two daughters. And while their skin was white and his was brown, it hadn't crossed little Paul's mind that they were anything other than his brother and sisters.

Denis was at high school and certainly acted like a big brother. He made the bigger boys let Paul join in their kickabouts on their street, and would rush to his rescue at the first sign of trouble. No one picked on Paul when Denis was around.

It didn't bother Paul for a second that all the other boys were at least two feet taller than he was. Soccer was fun! He would get stuck in just like the big boys, who quickly realised that a pint-sized Paul would fetch the ball back every time it rolled under a parked car. Their games lasted hours, ending only when the streetlights came on, and like clockwork, Mrs Donnelly would appear to call her boys in for bed.

For as long as he could remember, Paul had known his birth mother was out there somewhere in Dublin, but that she wasn't allowed to visit. Betty McGrath wasn't married when she had Paul and had to give him up when he was only a few weeks old. Sometimes he imagined what colour her eyes were or whether she smelled of apples like Mrs Donnelly. So when his foster mother told him his mammy was coming to visit at last, Paul's whole face lit up.

One morning, a woman arrived, carrying a little girl on her hip. The girl had the same colour skin as Paul, he noticed.

'Hello, Paul. I'm your mammy and this is Okune,' she said, introducing the two of them.

Paul was quiet. *Who was that girl?*

Betty took Paul to meet a friend. The friend had a little boy, Ernest, about Paul's age. They all went out for fish and chips on the pier – what a treat! Paul was warming to his mother already.

The next time Betty visited Paul, her partner and Okune's father, Pius came too. They walked to the Phoenix Park together. Betty had bought Paul a football made of thick orange plastic.

Paul traced his fingers along the grooves that made up the word 'WEMBLEY' in black letters. He couldn't read what it said, but he remembered something . . . Denis had a ball just like it!

Pius took the ball and crouched down. He rolled it a couple of metres towards Paul. 'Here you go, Paul. Kick it back to me.'

Paul was ready to show off all the skills that Denis had taught him on the street. He swung out his right foot, which connected perfectly with the centre of the ball.

Pius had to spring up quickly to catch it. 'That's it! The boy's got it!'

Watching on, Betty clapped her hands, beaming proudly.

An unfamiliar feeling surged through Paul's little body. He smiled back at Betty.

Not long after that, Paul went to stay with Betty, Pius and Okune. There were lots of tears when he left the Donnellys, but none of them belonged to Paul.

This is my new family now!

In the days that followed, Paul was happy. Then Pius went away and he didn't come back. Soon after, Betty announced they were going to visit Ernest. On the drive out of the city, Paul pressed his face to the car window excitedly, trying to catch glimpses of the sea. Soon, they arrived at a large stone building. Ivy had been allowed to creep up the high walls that surrounded it.

A lady was standing by to welcome them to 'The Bird's Nest' – and there was Ernest too! The boys played happily until it was time for Ernest to go home.

It was only then that Paul discovered that Betty had left too and he would be staying.

The orphanage in the coastal town of Dún Laoghaire would become Paul's home for the next few years. He would have liked to say he had some happy days there, but in truth they were marked by sadness. The fact that Paul looked different made him an easy target for some of the older children to bully him, while the staff were almost as mean.

And while 'The Bird's Nest' sounded like it should have been rooted in nature, there were no flowers, nor trees . . . not even a single blade of grass. The large grey yard made a gloomy playground.

The only time children were allowed to leave the grounds was to walk to school. Monkstown Primary School didn't have a uniform, but the children from The Bird's Nest were made to wear one anyway. Wearing scratchy blazers and horrible checked trousers, any child trying to run away would soon stick out in Dún Laoghaire.

Once enough time had passed to let Paul 'settle in', Betty began visiting again. His mother's betrayal was not easily forgotten, even when she tried to win him back with fizzy drinks, sweets and crisps. Hunger won out in the end, but what little food they were given each day was barely edible: greyish gruel for breakfast, fatty meat and bread as hard as The Nest's concrete yard. Reluctantly, Paul found himself looking forward to his mother's visits.

CHAPTER 3

THE GRASS OF GLENSILVA

The summer of 1971 brought big changes in Paul's life. Not only was he leaving primary school, but he was also swapping The Bird's Nest for Glensilva, another orphanage.

On the morning of his last day of primary school, Paul packed up what few bits and pieces he owned and took them with him in a box tied up with string. After school, he had to find his way to his new home, along with another couple of boys from The Nest. Paul felt glad he didn't have to turn up alone.

The large red-bricked house was set in a posh area of Dublin called Monkstown. It occupied a couple of acres and was set amongst other big houses with even bigger gardens.

Arriving at Glensilva, Paul was the new kid on the block again. Bigger bullies made his first days and months there miserable.

Paul tried to cling on to the small things to help him get through each day. The food at Glensilva was ten times better. The meat was edible and on the odd occasion, puddings were served. Apple tart or barmbrack . . . delicious! The dormitories were smaller too, with about half a dozen boys in each. There were no girls at all at Glensilva.

Most of all, Paul loved spending time outside in the gardens. At one side of the house was a large bumpy lawn that he and some of the other boys were allowed to turn into a pitch. It became his little sanctuary where he could escape for an hour or two with a ball.

Some of the boys also tried to get him to join in their games of Gaelic football, but he was never bothered. For Paul, it was 'soccer' all the way, as the sport was known in Ireland.

Whether it was lashing down with rain, or so hot that sweat soaked through his shirt, Paul would play on the grass of Glensilva for hours, only stopping from time to time for a quick gulp of water from the squeaky outdoor tap on the wall.

It was on that pitch where Paul began to make friends. Even the older boys were impressed with his solid skills.

In their five-a-side games, Paul seemed to be everywhere on the pitch! One moment, he was scooping up the ball in defence, the next he was outjumping his marker to plant a header, in between two jumpers used as goalposts.

Before long, the squabbling started. Whoever the team captains were that day would argue over who got first pick . . . and everyone knew that the team with Paul on it was bound to win!

It was a strange feeling to feel wanted, but Paul didn't let the attention go to his head.

That September, Paul began secondary school. Sallynoggin Vocational School, a Catholic school, was filled with children from the nearby housing estate on the Southside of Dublin. Paul tried to act tough like the boys from the 'Noggin', but he was easy prey for the bullies. He was the 'wrong' religion, from fancy Monkstown (if only they knew the truth about where he really lived) and Black. He was called horrible names because of the colour of his skin from the moment he arrived there.

Though it wasn't something he took pride in doing, Paul began fighting back. He and the other Glensilva lads formed a pack, ready to defend each other from anyone who thought they could pick a fight.

Everything changed when Paul decided to join in the games of soccer at breaktime. All they had to play with was a tennis ball, but that didn't seem to matter – about fifty boys all battled to win the ball on a chaotic concrete pitch.

There, Paul stood tall, showing the skills that he had practised every day at Glensilva, which quickly earned the respect of the boys from the estate. Once they had seen him with a ball at his feet, no one cared about what he looked like or where he lived. Almost overnight, the name-calling stopped, and he was Paul again.

'Paul, can you teach us how to do that turn?' one boy asked.

'I asked first!' said another.

Even the biggest Sallynoggin bullies were surprised when they discovered that Paul was even stronger than they were. Not one of them could knock him off the ball.

More wild games helped the boys eventually forge friendships. Before long, a few of the lads from the estate started coming up to Glensilva to play after school. It felt nice to have real friends, rather than just the boys at the orphanage.

Paul imagined a crowd of thousands of people cheering him on, and each match he played took him another step closer to achieving his dream of becoming a footballer one day.

CHAPTER 4

PEARSE ROVERS

At the weekends, some of Paul's classmates played for Pearse Rovers, a junior team in the Dublin and District Schoolboys League. Paul would listen keenly to their stories each Monday morning at school: a Pearse victory over a fierce rival or a ball-by-ball commentary of how one of them had scored a wondergoal.

Paul wished he could join them, and experience for himself what playing in a proper match was like.

'You should come down and play,' one of the Noggin boys said, encouragingly.

'Go on, Paul!' said another.

It wasn't Paul who needed convincing, though. It was Glensilva's housemaster, Mr Croxon, who was the stumbling block.

'I can't let you swan off to play soccer for hours, what would the other boys say?' Mr Croxon said, ruling out the possibility straight away.

So, for the time being, Paul had to make do with the kickabouts at school and in the gardens of Glensilva. All the while, his competitive streak and will to win grew stronger. Mr Croxon couldn't stop Paul from doing push-ups and sit-ups in the dormitory each day, or racing his friends to the shops on the bike that Betty had bought him. Paul would set himself little goals to achieve each week and would work on something even more energetic when he smashed his targets, which he almost always did.

When he wasn't exercising, Paul would be glued to the TV screen in the common room for all the big matches, along with a boy called Robert.

Paul and Robert had moved up from The Nest to Glensilva together. Robert was a Chelsea fan and taught Paul all about the club's big stars – Peter

Osgood, Charlie Cooke and Ron 'Chopper' Harris – until they became Paul's heroes too.

Paul used to beg Betty to bring him a football magazine on her visits, in the hope that there would be a poster of a Chelsea player inside to stick up on the dormitory wall.

The 1970 FA Cup final was a match that really captured the boys' imaginations. It was the first time that the final had been broadcast in colour, and Chelsea were playing Leeds United!

'Look how green the pitch is!' said Robert.

'And how blue Chelsea's shirts are!' added Paul excitedly.

They didn't even mind when the match was a draw and had to go to a replay, as it made Chelsea's win in extra time all the sweeter.

'Woo hoooo!' Paul and Robert cheered in delight.

After that, Paul began dreaming of pulling on the royal blue shirt of Chelsea. But it wouldn't be until his fourteenth birthday when he would finally get his hands on one – the first season that replica shirts were sold in shops.

Another of the Glensilva staff could see how much soccer meant to Paul. Mr Kennedy was from Northern Ireland and believed that the routine of training and playing matches each week might actually be good for Paul. He approached Mr Croxon and asked if Paul might be allowed to join Pearse Rovers.

This time, Mr Croxon agreed that Paul could go, but only for matches once a week.

It was better than nothing! Paul couldn't wait to get started.

The Rovers coach was a man called Tommy Heffernan. Tommy happily welcomed Paul into his under-12s team, but it quickly became clear that Paul would need a lot of training to bring him up to speed. Tennis ball soccer was all well and good, but the other boys had years of proper training under their belts by now, training that Paul had missed out on.

Paul didn't really understand how to beat the offside trap and was clueless when it came to playing in different formations. But when Tommy watched Paul in matches, it was clear the lad had plenty of potential. Unlike some of his boys, who charged about the pitch without much to show for their efforts, every pass Paul made was so calm and confident. Paul's reading of the game impressed the coach too; he was always a step or two ahead of his opponents. Not even Tommy could teach that.

'Don't worry, Paul. We'll make a player out of you yet!' Tommy reassured his new recruit.

Paul started Pearse's next match as centre-forward and went on to play in almost every position on the pitch until the time came for him to leave junior football behind at the age of eighteen.

In Paul's time as a Rover, the team never won much. Almost every cup and league was won by their Sallynoggin rivals Joey's, short for St Joseph's. One season, their coach even asked Paul whether he wanted to swap clubs.

'Sorry,' said Paul. 'But I belong at Pearse.' He wouldn't have swapped the time spent with his friends for all the trophies in Ireland!

CHAPTER 5

DALKEY DAYS

After years spent playing on scruffy schoolboys' pitches, Paul felt like he was dreaming when he moved up to his next club, Dalkey United. Here, there were neatly marked pitches, a goal with pristine nets at either end and a clubhouse that put the tin-can shed at Rovers to shame.

The best thing about Dalkey, though, were his teammates, who included his good friend 'Gramps' from Glensilva and some of his old schoolmates from Sallynoggin.

Paul found the matches in Dalkey's league a lot more competitive, which suited him just fine. Eighteen now, Paul stood at six-feet tall, and he could rival anyone on the pitch for speed and strength. Over that first season, Paul was on impressive form, switching between right-back and centre-back.

'Wherever you need me, boss!' he told his new coach Frank Mullen keenly.

Another man who worked at the club was Billy Behan. Billy had once been a footballer himself, a goalkeeper for Shamrock Rovers, before a brief spell at the great Manchester United. Now Billy worked as a scout for the English club, scouring the Irish leagues to bring the best young talent to Manchester.

Billy wasn't the only one checking out promising players. Scouts from all the big English clubs would turn up from time to time, including at Paul's first match in Dalkey colours.

Paul was more than ready for his Dalkey debut and had polished his boots for the occasion. Their opposition was a German side called Wattenscheid. Playing a team from across the seas in Europe felt special.

'This is what it must feel like to be an international footballer!' Paul said to Gramps. In his head, Paul pretended he was playing for Ireland against West Germany at the World Cup.

A good crowd had gathered at Dalkey's Hyde Road ground, from Dublin and beyond. Paul stood out to the scouts that day for three reasons: his height, the colour of his skin, at a time when there were far fewer Black people living in Ireland, and his amazing ability with a football.

On that cold and windy Dublin day, Paul ran rings around his German opponents while barely breaking a sweat! In fact, he was streets ahead of all the other twenty-one players on the pitch.

Billy Behan nudged Coach Frank as Paul came off the pitch. 'That kid's going to Old Trafford, mark my words!'

But nothing was said to Paul. One match didn't make a Division One player!

Every time Paul played, he would look out for Billy and the other scouts on the sidelines. Signing for a big English club was the dream of almost every young Irish footballer!

Paul's move to Dalkey wasn't the only big shift in his life – lots changed in his late teenage years. His schooldays ended when his teachers' patience finally ran out and he was expelled from the Noggin. By then, he was barely turning up to class, so it didn't come as too much of a surprise.

He also left the care of his final children's home, Racefield House, and now had a room in a flat in Dublin's Southside, a couple of miles from where Dalkey played. The staff at the club helped Paul find work. He juggled various jobs with his time spent playing football, as a slater, a warehouse man, even a nightwatchman. Having money in his pocket for the first time made Paul feel free.

Another big milestone was Paul's first trip outside of Ireland, when Dalkey travelled to play Wattenscheid for the return fixture. He was excited, he had never been on a plane before!

Paul played well during his days in Germany but found the nights there much more difficult. Off the pitch, he was desperately shy and was less independent than other teenagers his age. Many of his Dalkey teammates were much older, and some had families of their own. Paul was glad when it was time to go home to Dublin.

Dalkey's first match back was against Dunleary Celtic in Ballynoggin, and it was during this match that a clash of heads left him feeling dizzy. That was two bumps to the head now, after an earlier knock in Germany. Thinking nothing of it, Paul played on.

At home that evening though, Paul started acting oddly and began saying strange things. What was real and what was only in his head began to blur. He didn't feel frightened, but he didn't understand what was happening to him.

His flatmate made a frantic phone call. Something was very wrong with Paul, and the next thing he knew, he was being driven away in an ambulance.

Paul spent the next twelve months recovering in St Vincent's Hospital. At first, the doctors said that Paul was too poorly for visitors. His medicine made him sleep for most of the day and he couldn't talk or eat by himself.

As soon as they were allowed, Betty and Okune came to visit. They would sit with Paul for hours, not knowing if he could hear a word they were saying, but they kept showing up.

Paul wanted to speak, but no words would come out. If he had been able, he would have told his mother and sister how they made him feel safe, as two guardian angels by his side.

Frank Mullen and Paul's friends from Dalkey wanted to help too. 'Don't you worry, Paul,' they told him. 'Your place on the team will be waiting when you feel well again.'

It was a long road, but over time, Paul began to feel like himself again. Finally, the doctors agreed that Betty could take him home.

Sadly, though, things got worse before they got better. Paul hadn't been at home for long before he fell ill again. He was back in a hospital bed for months and became very thin and weak. Doctors warned that he might never walk again.

Still, Paul's friends and family didn't give up on his chances of recovery. Over time, he proved the doctors wrong and began shuffling small steps across his room, but he never said a word.

More weeks passed. Sometimes, Paul's friends from Dalkey took him for walks in the garden. Gramps had the idea of taking a football in the hope that it might help to break Paul out of his trance. He rolled the ball along the ground to Paul, who lurched forwards and missed. Gramps wasn't sure if Paul could even see the football.

One day, a new nurse started working on the ward. She came into Paul's room with fresh sheets for his bed and got talking with Betty.

'Paul's a footballer,' Betty introduced her son. 'He's going to play at Wembley someday.'

Suddenly, Paul's eyes lit up. And for the first time in a long time, he managed a little smile.

Gramps kept bringing his football until Paul learned how to kick it again. Eventually, Paul was back in a pair of boots and training with Dalkey. His doctors were amazed by his recovery. No one at the club spoke about Paul's lost months in hospital, terrified it might set him back. They thought the best treatment was to get him back on a football pitch, the place where Paul had been happy.

CHAPTER 6

THE BLACK PEARL OF INCHICORE

In 1980, Paul felt strong enough to return to match action with Dalkey. Soon, the big defender was back on the scouts' radars too. One day, there were whispers that a scout from Tottenham Hotspur had come to see him play.

'You wouldn't sign for Spurs now, would you, Paul? Not with you being a Chelsea fan, and all,' Gramps teased.

'I could be tempted!' Paul replied.

The lure of playing at White Hart Lane would have really tested Paul's loyalty, but no offer came in from Spurs.

So, Paul decided to concentrate on the season ahead with Dalkey. The team's first match of the season was against their noisy Dublin neighbours Fatima.

There wasn't much to report from the match until late on, when Paul's last-ditch tackle made one of the Fatima forwards look silly. Paul had come out of nowhere to win the ball just as his opponent was pulling back his leg to shoot!

When he didn't win a foul for the challenge, the Fatima player began hurling abuse at Paul and laughing with his teammates. Usually, Paul took moments like this in his stride, but this time the name-calling was based on the colour of his skin.

Without thinking, Paul kicked out at his opponent. A clear foul! He regretted his actions straight away and trudged off the pitch without bothering to wait for the ref's red card.

Dalkey were ordered to pay a fine of £3, which they refused flat out. Paying it would send the wrong message: that players could get away with racist comments. It felt good that Dalkey were always on Paul's side.

In 1981, Paul was chosen to play in the Oscar Traynor Cup Final, as part of the Leinster Senior League side that defeated County Mayo. Paul's performance over ninety minutes easily made him Player of the Match. Even a fair-weather fan could see that Paul's tackling, heading, distribution and reading of the game that day was leagues above anyone else.

A man called Charlie Walker, the manager of St Patrick's Athletic, thought so too. His club played at Richmond Park in Inchicore, Dublin. They weren't one of the giants of the Irish league like Shamrock Rovers or Dundalk, but they had some strong players in their team of semi-pros.

Walker was looking for a treasure he could polish into a League of Ireland player, and in Paul, he had discovered a gem. Straight after that final, he went to talk to Frank Mullen.

The following morning, after saying some sad goodbyes to everyone at Dalkey, Paul became a St Pat's player. For the first time, he would get paid to play football! It wasn't enough to give up his job, but it was one step closer to his dream of becoming a professional footballer.

Walker decided to play Paul as a striker, and he did score a few goals in a red shirt, but only after switching to the heart of the St Pat's defence did Paul really shine.

Paul got a kick out of seeing his name printed in the matchday programme, which he saved for his mother each game. Betty also collected all of Paul's newspaper clippings from his matches in the League of Ireland. One journalist soon nicknamed Paul 'The Black Pearl of Inchicore', the rarest treasure St Pat's had ever discovered. Paul's reputation was growing with each match he played.

One day, a special visitor from Manchester came over to watch Paul's game. Sir Matt Busby had been Manchester United's legendary manager in the 1950s and 60s and was now the club president. He knew football inside out.

St Pat's had made Paul and his old coach at Dalkey United a promise – that if a big club ever came in for Paul, they wouldn't stand in his way. Now, they had to keep that promise . . .

'I've a bit of news for you, Paul . . .' said Walker, a few days after Matt Busby's visit. 'United want you in Manchester on a month's trial.'

'A bit of news!' thought Paul. This was information that could change Paul's life forever!

More offers came in for the young defender that same week, from Manchester City, Luton Town and Watford. What was going on? His short time as a Saint had been an absolute whirlwind!

Paul felt flattered that four English clubs wanted to sign him, but deciding his next move was an easy one.

'I'll take the trial at Manchester United,' he told Walker.

Paul's teammates decided to celebrate by holding a goodbye party for Paul. They were all good footballers, but Paul had a star quality that the others could only dream of.

'That trial's in the bag, no doubt about it!' said Gramps.

CHAPTER 7

MOVING TO MANCHESTER

'I'm Norman,' a long-legged teenager said, holding out his hand.

'Paul McGrath,' Paul replied shyly.

Norman Whiteside was from Northern Ireland and was another of Manchester United's recent recruits. He was only sixteen, but stood even taller than Paul, and could easily have passed for mid-twenties. Norman had the room above in the digs Paul was staying in during his trial, in the Chorlton area of Manchester, not far from where Sir Matt lived.

The lads hit it off immediately, and Paul was glad to have Norman around to show him the ropes at United. Although Norman was six years younger than

Paul, he was twice as confident. He never blushed red when one of the first-team players passed them in the corridor or went jelly-legged when Atkinson turned up at the side of the pitch.

During their first few training sessions together, Paul's nerves kept bubbling to the surface. Each time he made a bobbly pass or was outjumped in a header, he would doubt himself.

'Relax!' said Norman. 'They wouldn't have asked you here if they didn't want you.'

Paul desperately wanted to believe him. He didn't want to go back to welding metal – he wanted to be a professional footballer more than anything!

Then came Paul's chance to prove himself. His first appearance in a red shirt would be for Manchester United's reserves, in a match against Newcastle United.

'I told you so!' said Norman, when he saw Paul's name alongside his own on the teamsheet.

And for the first time since arriving in Manchester, Paul managed a huge smile.

While Paul and Norman were building a good friendship off the pitch, they worked well together on it, too. Midway through the match, Paul launched a clearance from his own box all the way to the Newcastle box. Nothing special, or so he thought. But there was Norman in the perfect place to collect the pass. The ball bounced once, then – *SMASH!* – he crashed home a fantastic half-volley.

'That was one heck of a pass, Macca!' Norman raved, after the match.

Paul scratched his head. It was Norman who had done all the work!

After playing a couple more reserve matches, Atkinson had seen enough. This big centre-half from Dublin had something about him.

'The boy's a little rough around the edges, but we've got to keep him,' Atkinson told the club chairman.

So a contract was drafted, ready for Paul to sign.

But when Paul read it through in Atkinson's office, he almost spat out his drink of water.

Just £101 a week? He was making more than that in Dublin, playing for St Pat's and from his latest job as a metal worker! It hardly seemed generous for a club the size of Manchester United!

Paul asked politely if Atkinson could up the money. 'Soccer is my dream, but I was thinking it might pay a little more than that.'

'That's our offer. Take it or leave it.' Atkinson wasn't budging.

Twenty-two years old was rather late to be starting out as a professional footballer, and a chance like this might not come along again. Paul knew it and Atkinson knew it. There weren't many who turned down the famous Manchester United.

'Where do I sign?' Paul said at last.

Atkinson handed Paul a pen, who scribbled his signature on the dotted line. Then they shook hands on the deal.

'Now take that awful thing out of your ear . . . how many great centre-halves do you know that wear earrings?' huffed Atkinson.

Paul reached for his ear, twiddled the stud and put it in his pocket. Problem solved.

'And one more thing,' barked Atkinson, as Paul was halfway out of the door. 'It's "football" here, never "soccer".'

At that moment, Paul could never have imagined that Atkinson would become one of the biggest supporters of Paul's career. Atkinson was acting like he couldn't stand him!

Norman was waiting downstairs at the Cliff training ground. 'How did it go?' he asked excitedly.

Paul told him everything, about the contract and the earring.

'Ah, have you seen the gold on his fingers? He probably wants the earring for himself!' Norman joked. 'Welcome to United!'

With the season nearing an end, Atkinson was making future plans. Half the squad were away on international duty at the World Cup that summer, which left a space to bring Paul on the club's pre-season tour to North America.

When Atkinson shared the news, Paul couldn't believe his luck. Travelling to cities like Vancouver, San Diego and Seattle with the first team . . . he felt slightly star-struck! This was the biggest opportunity of his life!

Sadly though, he didn't make the tour. A bad tackle

from a Sheffield United striker, in one of the very last reserve matches of the season, meant that Paul had to stay behind in England to have an operation on his knee. *Aaarghh!* The timing was terrible!

So far as a footballer, although he'd had a terrible head injury, he hadn't injured his limbs, so to have an operation sounded serious. Little did he know it was to be the first of many surgeries on his poor knees.

Paul went home to Crumlin that summer to recover, and spent a happy few weeks watching the World Cup on TV with his family. There was no Republic of Ireland team to follow – they hadn't managed to qualify – but Northern Ireland had made it to Spain '82. Paul decided to adopt them for the tournament . . . their star player was none other than his new friend Norman Whiteside, who was taking on the world aged seventeen!

CHAPTER 8

CHALK AND CHEESE

Paul's knee operation was a success and before long, he was pushing for a place in the first team again.

When it came to mixing with Man United's superstars in the changing room or the canteen at the Cliff, though, Paul struggled to make conversation with anyone but Norman. Instead, he let his feet do the talking on the pitch, where he was getting better and better and better.

Before long, Atkinson decided Paul was ready to make his Division One debut. Paul showed no signs of nerves against Tottenham Hotspur. Playing with the big boys in front of a cheering Old Trafford crowd was exactly where he wanted to be!

But with so many strong players ahead of him, Paul's progress wasn't quite as rapid as his pace. At the time, each team was only allowed to name one substitute, which made getting a run of games in the first team an almost impossible task. Consequently, Paul kept working hard behind the scenes, so he'd be ready for action if others were ever out injured or suspended.

In 1983, Paul knew he wasn't in the team when Manchester United reached the FA Cup final, but he happily travelled down to Wembley to cheer on the boys. He still got to walk on the Wembley pitch before the match and join in the celebrations when United paraded the trophy on an open-top bus that season.

It was all good practice for two years later, when Paul had cemented his place in Atkinson's first eleven, and this time he battled through 120 minutes to lift the same trophy for himself. Now he was a superstar footballer, too!

In Paul's first four seasons playing under Atkinson, Manchester United had won two FA Cups and never finished lower than fourth in the league. Not bad! The style of football which Atkinson encouraged in his team delighted the fans, but the bosses wanted more. Their Number One goal was to win the league.

United's start to the 1986–87 season did little to suggest that this was going to be their year. Before October had begun, Atkinson's side had already suffered six worrying defeats in the league. In November they crashed out of the League Cup too, embarrassingly beaten 4–1 in a replay down at Southampton.

Just two days later, Atkinson was given the big heave-ho. The club statement read that he had 'lost the confidence of the players'.

Not true! thought Paul. For him, Atkinson had been a brilliant boss. He might have pinched the pennies over Paul's contract, but he was a passionate football manager who treated his players with respect and affection to get the best out of them. Paul was sorry to see Atkinson go.

Atkinson's replacement was Scottish manager Alex Ferguson. He arrived in Manchester having won a

European trophy, after his Aberdeen side incredibly beat Spanish giants Real Madrid.

Manchester United midfielder Gordon Strachan had been part of Aberdeen's cup-winning side. He warned his teammates about Ferguson's impossible standards and his fiery temper.

'He sounds nothing at all like Atkinson,' Paul whispered to Norman.

After a few training sessions, it was painfully clear that Ferguson wanted to run a tight ship. He was shocked to learn that first-team players including Paul, Norman and the club captain Bryan Robson liked to stay out late partying when they should have been resting their bodies.

'We can't possibly compete with teams like Liverpool if we're not in the best shape!' Ferguson said, disciplining his team.

'Yes, Mr Ferguson,' the players replied half-heartedly.

They had a choice . . . pull their socks up and work hard for the team, or be booted out to other clubs.

'I won't have any bad apples in my squad,' Ferguson warned.

So, for the rest of the season, Paul knuckled down to training at the Cliff. He and Norman still snuck out for late nights – luckily for them without the manager finding out. No one wanted to be blasted by Ferguson's 'hairdryer treatment', a form of telling-off that had become legendary.

That season, Paul kept on being picked for Ferguson's side, playing forty games in all. He still got a kick each time he pulled on the famous red shirt of Manchester United, although he was loving life a little less with Ferguson running the show.

As for Manchester United, they didn't become title contenders overnight, ending the season in eleventh place. Ferguson warned the players there would be big changes at the club.

Paul and Norman breathed a sigh of relief not to find their names on the transfer list as the season neared its end; neither player was ready to move on just yet. On paper, there was no real reason for Ferguson to get rid of them . . . both players were internationals by now, with their best years of their careers likely still ahead of them.

CHAPTER 9

THE BOY IN GREEN

Unlike his good friend Norman, Paul didn't exactly burst on to the international scene. It wasn't until his third season with Manchester United, in 1985, that he was called up for Ireland by manager Eoin Hand. By then he was twenty-five. Hand had first met Paul at St Patrick's, the club Hand now managed when he wasn't on Ireland duty.

Ireland had a strong squad with players like Liam Brady, Mark Lawrenson, David O'Leary, and with Paul's United teammates Kevin Moran and Frank Stapleton in their ranks. Paul knew he had his work cut out for him to break into the side.

Hand's phone call had come like a bolt out of the

blue. Paul's early excitement had since been overtaken by feelings of worry.

'What does Hand want with me?' he confided in Kevin at the Cliff. 'Those lads must have hundreds of caps between them.'

Kevin smiled. 'Just go and enjoy yourself, Macca. Everything will be grand.'

Kevin was right, Paul did enjoy himself. In fact, he loved his first training session with the Boys in Green!

Later that night, though, Paul almost ended his international career before it had even begun! The new boy didn't know he was supposed to stay in the team hotel with all the other players and instead went to his mother's house in Crumlin after training. Hand was furious when Paul finally appeared the next morning but decided to let slip Paul's honest mistake.

Dalymount Park was a stadium squeezed between rows of terraced houses on Dublin's Northside. It was set to be packed to the rafters for Ireland's match that day, as world champions Italy were visiting to play a friendly!

In truth, too many tickets were sold. Fans spilled

so close to the sidelines that sliding tackles had to be ruled out altogether. And the atmosphere felt even more special than at Old Trafford.

Paul felt lucky to be named on the bench that night. It was one of the best seats in the house! Just watching legends like Liam was an honour, while Italy still had the core of the team that had won the World Cup in 1982 on show.

There were only ten minutes on the ref's stopwatch when Paul was called unexpectedly into action. Defender Mark Lawrenson had injured his shoulder and couldn't play on.

A pang of anxiety flashed through Paul's body. 'You sure about this, boss?' he asked, his brow suddenly beading with sweat. 'Can Mark not run it off?'

'Don't be silly, Paul, they're taking him straight to Jervis Street Hospital!' said Hand.

So, Paul unzipped his tracksuit top and jogged to the touchline.

In the end, Italy showed why they were world champions, winning the game 2–1 with goals from Paolo Rossi and Alessandro Altobelli. Ireland had made it a good contest, though, even treating the fans to a goal from Gary Waddock. As for Paul, he hadn't put a foot wrong since coming on.

After that, Paul started the next two international friendlies, but was taken off at half-time against England at Wembley.

'You can't just switch off when you feel like it, Paul,' Hand told him. 'Not against players like Bryan Robson and Gary Lineker.'

Paul nodded, taking on the advice carefully. He was learning all the time.

The whole nation dreamed of reaching their first World Cup, so it came as a blow when Ireland didn't qualify for the 1986 tournament. They only had themselves to blame, with too many poor results to make it to Mexico. What made matters worse was that their neighbours Northern Ireland *had* qualified for a second time, after finishing as runners-up in their group, behind England.

The bosses at Ireland weren't happy. With the talented players they had in their own squad, they saw it as an opportunity missed. Hand was given his marching orders and the search for a new manager began.

It was tough staying at home that summer, but Paul still tuned into every match as a fan. This was the World Cup, after all, the biggest sporting competition on the planet! The first tournament that had Paul hooked was Brazil 1970, when the Brazilians had played some incredible football that year to lift their third title. Gerson, Jairzinho and Pelé at the height of his powers . . . the skill on show made Paul's jaw gape wide. Until then, Paul had only known the heroics of the all-white England team that had won the 1966 trophy. The Brazil players looked like Paul!

That could be me one day, Paul had dared to dream.

Fast forward to 1986 and the team that he was following most closely was Northern Ireland, his best friend Norman's team. Norman was still only twenty-one, but had made a name for himself at the tournament in Spain, when he'd broken Pelé's record to become the youngest player at a World Cup, aged seventeen years and forty-one days.

Paul cheered on Norman in the three matches

he played, but Northern Ireland didn't make the knockouts. In a group that included Brazil and hosts Spain, it was an impossible task.

Back in Manchester, Norman shared his World Cup stories with Paul and some of the other lads. Paul hung off his every word.

'It sounds incredible,' he said to Norman.

Paul could only imagine how proud he would feel to play for his country in a top tournament. It wouldn't be easy, but Paul made it his next goal.

CHAPTER 10

JACK'S LAD

In February 1986, Jack Charlton was hired as the man to change Ireland's fortunes. As a player, he had won the World Cup with England, before managing three different clubs in the north of England.

The bosses at the Irish Football Association knew they were taking a risk in bringing in Charlton. Never before had someone born outside of Ireland been given the top job. If it backfired, the fans would be on the Irish FA's back. In the end, the bosses decided it was a risk worth taking, and Charlton teamed up with Ireland in time to lead their Euro 1988 qualification campaign.

Charlton hoped to build Ireland's strongest squad yet, and cast his net wide in the search for fresh talent. The 'Granny Rule' they called it: if a player had Irish parents or grandparents, but was born in, say, England or Scotland, they were allowed to play for the Republic. In came Liverpool pair Ray Houghton and John Aldridge, midfielder Andy Townsend and forward Tony Cascarino.

Paul, meanwhile, was in Charlton's first squads too. He was a little laid-back for Charlton's liking, but the new coach quickly came to admire Paul's perfect positioning and timely tackles. Before Charlton's first match as boss of the Boys in Green, he even asked Paul to stand in as skipper for their upcoming friendly.

'John,' Charlton began. 'I want you in midfield against Wales. Oh, and you're the captain.'

Paul froze. *Midfield, sure, but John's not my name . . . and I definitely can't be captain!*

It was hard enough looking after himself, let alone having to organise all the other lads. The responsibility was just too big.

Paul confided in injured captain Frank Stapleton and Liam Brady. 'I can't be captain. I just want to do my own job well.'

Frank and Liam understood. 'We'll tell the gaffer,' they promised.

After that, Paul was sometimes known by Charlton as 'John', and sometimes as 'James', but at least he never had to be captain. He wondered if Charlton *did* know his name after all and was just teasing him the whole time!

Whether Charlton knew Paul's name or not, he nevertheless came to rely on his skills as a player in Ireland's important European qualifiers that followed. Charlton could have played him anywhere, centre-back, midfield, right-back . . . although goalkeeper might have been a stretch.

Results in qualification were mixed. Priceless points were won on the road in Belgium and Scotland, but both fixtures ended goalless back at Lansdowne Road. And with their away defeat to Bulgaria, Ireland's Euros hopes were looking dangerously slim. Now they would have to beat Bulgaria and hope that Scotland could do them a favour by beating the Bulgarians the following month too!

Paul was convinced the boys were just playing for pride when they hosted Bulgaria. It was a fine performance, with a goal from Paul and another from Kevin, before the brilliant Liam was sent off late on. Eleven points earned, but likely not enough to take top spot. It would be a nervous month's wait to discover their fate, decided when Scotland travelled to Sofia in November 1987.

Paul was just coming around from another knee operation late one evening, at Manchester's Whalley Range Hospital, when he heard the happy news.

Feeling groggy, the newsreader's words swirled around in his head. 'Scotland . . . Bulgaria . . . Jack Charlton . . . Ireland . . .'

Slowly, Paul began to piece the words together like a puzzle. *No, we can't have? Can we?*

Suddenly, the phone on his bedside locker began to buzz.

'Would you believe it? Scotland have beaten Bulgaria!' said Kevin's excited voice. 'We've only gone and done it . . . WE'RE GOING TO THE EUROS!'

Paul's excited scream was so loud, the nurses must have thought he had fallen out of bed!

As the tournament grew closer, though, doubts began to creep into Paul's mind. His recovery from his knee operation had been long and painful.

What if my body lets me down in Germany? he worried.

The day before they were due to leave for Germany, Paul was beginning to panic. In Ireland's final session on the training pitch, he shared a secret with Kevin.

'I've changed my mind,' he said. 'I don't want to go to the Euros.'

Kevin laughed, but his face changed when he realised Paul wasn't messing around.

'Okay, Paul,' Kevin said, playing along. 'How about we see how you feel in the morning before telling the boss.'

Kevin didn't tell a soul, hoping it was just a wobble. Paul was fast becoming one of Ireland's most important players! Thankfully, Paul changed his mind again and packed his suitcase for Germany along with the rest of the team.

CHAPTER 11

THE ROAD TO WEST GERMANY

For many of Ireland's travelling fans, the European Championship in West Germany would be a trip of a lifetime. Thousands of them had never set foot out of the country, and so a scramble for passports followed. Irish officials worked around the clock, while the fans anxiously checked their letterboxes each morning.

In 1988, the days of low-cost flights were still years away, so the route to the tournament for many was epic. A ferry over the Irish Sea to Holyhead, a drive east across England to board another ferry to Belgium next, before driving more hours on the opposite side of the road to reach to their destination in West

Germany. With every car and van proudly bearing the Ireland tricolour, it was the greatest road trip ever!

Expectations were high as Charlton's squad headed to Germany. It may have been Ireland's first big tournament, but they weren't just going to make up the numbers. Every player in the squad of twenty believed. And while they hadn't as many big-name players as the English, Dutch or Italians, they were a decent side who were willing to give everything for each other.

After Paul had turned down the chance to be captain, Frank Stapleton was trusted to keep the armband. Paul was pleased to see it go to his old United teammate, as Frank had a way of making every player feel important.

'On our day, we can beat anyone!' the skipper told his team, to huge cheers.

Ireland's first ever match at a European Championship was as big as they came. They would make their bow against rivals England at the Stuttgart Arena.

England's side was stuffed with superstars. Paul's Manchester United captain Bryan 'Robbo' Robson led the Three Lions in Germany too, John Barnes and Chris Waddle worked the wings, Glenn Hoddle and Peter Beardsley were gifted midfielders, while Gary Lineker had shone at the World Cup two years earlier, winning the Golden Boot.

So, when underdogs Ireland took a shock lead after six minutes, there were as many gasps from fans in green shirts as from those wearing white! Even little Ray Houghton seemed surprised to score, when he nodded a header past goalkeeper Peter Shilton from John Aldridge's flick-on.

The England players were also stunned, and spent the rest of the half in a daze. Then when Ronnie Whelan hit the bar for Ireland, England were spared more blushes!

While most of the Irish players felt on top of the world, half-time couldn't come too soon enough for Paul. His knee had been throbbing ever since he'd attempted a shot early on.

'You've got to sub me,' Paul begged the staff.

But without the injured Liam Brady, left at home in Ireland, the team didn't have a back-up that could run the midfield the way Paul could.

'We need you on that pitch,' Charlton ordered. 'End of.'

Paul grimaced. He knew there was no point arguing with the boss. He would have to find a way to play through the pain.

Meanwhile, manager Bobby Robson used the break to put a rocket up his England side. The second half saw Ireland's opponents come out fired up. On three occasions Gary Lineker was put through on goal: first he was denied by a point-blank save from Pat Bonner, next he clipped the crossbar and third, the striker dragged his shot wide. It just wasn't his day!

Barnes, Beardsley and Robson all had chances too, each one snuffed out by a sensational save from the Irish keeper!

'You'll have to do better than that to beat our Pat,' Kevin Moran teased his Man United teammate Bryan Robson.

'Challenge accepted!' Robbo replied.

England kept pummelling Pat's goal, but they couldn't find a way past Ireland's Number 1. He was having the game of his life!

At the other end, John came close to adding a second Irish goal just moments before it was all over. Thankfully, his miss didn't matter. What a win! The mighty England had been humbled. It felt fantastic to get the better of their old enemy!

Kevin put an arm around Paul and helped him hobble off the pitch as a hero. 'And to think you didn't want to come to Germany!'

Paul just laughed. He'd forgotten he'd even said it!

CHAPTER 12

AN EPIC EUROS

After playing all ninety minutes against England, Paul could barely stand up straight. This time, even Charlton agreed that his midfielder would have to sit out their next game – against the Soviet Union – in Hanover. So, Paul sat in the stands with an icepack strapped to his injured knee.

The game was one Paul would have loved to play in. Ireland showed everyone they were more than just a 'hit and hope' side, playing some fantastic football to outclass the Soviets. If the score had ended Ireland 4–1 Soviet Union, it would have been hard to argue it wasn't a fair result. Sadly though, Ireland could only make one of their chances count.

It was a beautiful goal that saw Paul forget all about his painful knee for a moment: a long throw reached Ronnie Whelan on the edge of the box, who smashed home an amazing acrobatic volley

Goooooaaaaalllll!

They didn't need me, after all! thought Paul.

All was going well for Ireland until midway through the second half, when after a period of pressure, the Soviet striker Oleh Protasov put an equaliser through Pat's legs.

The goalkeeper slammed his glove to the ground in disgust!

With four points from two games, Ireland needed a result against their next opponents, the Netherlands. The Dutch desperately needed points too. So far, they just had three, having lost to the Soviets before bouncing back in style to smash England. If they beat Ireland too, the team in orange would be in the final four.

'A draw will be good enough to see us through to the semis, so no need to try anything fancy,' Charlton warned his players. Above all else, he wanted his team to stay solid at the back, and then who knew – they might just nick a goal from a counterattack.

By now, Paul had been patched up and was back in the team. He listened carefully to Charlton's words and nodded in agreement. He understood that while Ireland may not play the most attractive style of football, it was what had got them to the Euros.

The rest of the team bought into Charlton's tactics that day, too. And the fans didn't mind one bit. Everyone knew that the Netherlands team boasted some seriously skilled young players. They had Ruud Gullit and Frank Rijkaard, not to mention the flying Dutchman Marco van Basten, who had just hit a hat-trick that had ended England's Euros.

The Netherlands enjoyed plenty of possession early on, with Pat Bonner tested by strikes from Adri van Tiggelen and Jan Wouters. Then it was Ireland's turn to attack. In the fifteenth minute, a corner was swung into the box and Paul leapt magnificently to meet it. The ball slammed powerfully against the post before it was cleared off the line and scrambled away!

'How did that stay out?' Paul moaned desperately.

Half-time came, with Paul switching to right-back for the injured Chris Morris after that. The Netherlands players weren't giving up, peppering Pat's goal with shot after shot. It wasn't until the eighty-third minute that Ireland's defensive heroics were finally undone, when what can only be described as a freak goal was scored.

Paul had bravely headed away yet another Dutch shot but could only direct the ball into the path of Ronald Koeman. Koeman drove a fierce volley straight into the ground, which bounced up and into the box. The ball was spinning wildly as it landed on the head of substitute Wim Kieft, and kept on spinning past Pat's left glove and inside the far post.

Goooooaaaaalllll!

Ireland were down and out, while the Dutch lived to fight another day.

Paul was devastated. The boys had come so close to the semis. Their team spirit had been unbreakable over the past three matches. After the England victory, he honestly thought Ireland would go on to compete for the trophy.

One fluky goal from the Dutch, though, did nothing to change how the Irish fans felt about their team. In the supporters' eyes, the Boys in Green were heroes and deserved unlimited applause. And they hadn't forgotten the manager – Charlton was adopted as Ireland's newest national hero! Half an hour after full time, the fans were still singing and chanting the players' names, enjoying some last few magical moments before beginning the long journey home.

Ireland's plane touched down at Dublin airport the next day to be greeted by thousands of well-wishers, flags and banners. Most of the players loved the limelight and stopped happily for photos or to sign an autograph.

'Ooh aah, Paul McGrath!' The fans had even made up a chant for their new hero!

But Paul slipped away as soon as he could, happy for others to take centre stage. Even though he had put in two strong performances, he couldn't shake the feeling that he had somehow let down the fans.

Imagine their faces if we'd come home as champions! he thought to himself.

Now there was something to aim for! There was time for more tournaments yet . . . Paul's journey with the national side was only just beginning.

CHAPTER 13

AN UNEASY EXIT

During the season before the 1988 Euros, Paul's troublesome knees had forced him to sit out almost five months, while Norman had joined him as a long-term patient on the treatment table. The injuries had come as a blow, but without them, Alex Ferguson had managed to steer Manchester United to second place, with new signings Steve Bruce and Viv Anderson soon settling into the United defence.

Both Paul and Norman were still convinced they were for the chopping block, but it was Irish defender Kevin Moran who was sold at the end of the season, after serving the club for a whole decade.

Ahead of the 1988–89 season, Paul returned to Manchester to tackle his seventh season as a Red Devil. This was Ferguson's second full season in charge and the big bosses awaited a trophy impatiently. The biggest signing that summer was Mark Hughes, who returned from Barcelona for £1.8 million, a club record fee. The fans were thrilled, believing that Mark was exactly the player to boost United's strike force.

In the first half of the new season, Mark was keeping up his end of the bargain by scoring in almost every match in the league. At the back though, their defence was leaking goals, which saw the team drop down to the middle of the table.

Paul returned from yet another injury on New Year's Day 1989, just in time for a huge league clash with champions Liverpool. All Paul's begging had paid off, and Ferguson put him back in the United defence! Paul played ninety minutes in a 3–1 win that lifted the Red Devils to sixth place. His comeback didn't last long though, as his knee was too badly swollen to play in their next match, an FA Cup tie.

With Norman sidelined too, the pair decided to go partying instead of staying at home to recover. That was the final straw for Ferguson. Paul was making him look bad, the club look bad, and he didn't seem to care about his own career.

'It's time for a meeting with Mr McGrath,' Ferguson told his assistant, Archie Knox.

Paul probably should have read the signs, but he went into the meeting expecting nothing more than another dressing-down.

Instead, Ferguson presented Paul with a proposal out of nowhere. If Paul retired quietly and went back to Ireland, the club would pay him £100,000 and put on a testimonial game in his honour.

Paul gasped. *Retire?* He'd had his fair share of injuries by now, but at twenty-nine, he was years off hanging up his boots. It made no sense.

What Paul didn't know is that Liverpool had made an offer for the defender. United would never agree to sell him to their bitter rivals and kept it a secret. Instead, the club decided they could convince Paul to retire from the game altogether. Of course, if Paul had known, he would have swapped one red shirt for another in a heartbeat!

Paul left the meeting feeling knocked for six: 'I'll need some time to think about it.'

The amount of money United were offering wasn't a small sum – enough to buy a huge house in Ireland – but it would hardly make him a millionaire. By now, he had a wife and two young sons to think about.

Paul talked it over with his closest teammates, who were just as shocked as Paul.

'They can't do that!' said a horrified Norman.

'You shouldn't accept it,' Robbo agreed.

So Paul turned down Manchester United's offer. He didn't feel anywhere near ready to stop playing the game he loved.

'They can throw me out of the club, but there's no way I'm quitting football!' he told his friends.

When Ron Atkinson found out, he tried to bring Paul to Sheffield Wednesday, the club where he was now in charge. Atkinson made Man United a good offer, but the club was holding out for more money.

The very next day, Aston Villa came in with a strong bid of £425,000. Boss Graham Taylor was desperate to bring Paul to Villa Park. So Paul and his wife Claire found themselves on a train to Birmingham to talk things over.

Unlike United, Villa made Paul an offer he couldn't refuse. If he joined the club, they would triple his wages! Furthermore, Taylor seemed much more like the sort of manager Paul could see himself playing for – so Paul signed for Aston Villa, hoping for a fresh start.

Sadly, though, Paul's problems soon followed him from Manchester. In his first season as a Villan, his damaged knees still limited the number of matches he played, and he was struggling off the pitch too.

Leaving Manchester had been a big change for Paul, and he wasn't coping well. He felt rejected by his old club, the same feeling of rejection that kept rearing its ugly head his whole life. He fell into a deep spiral and ended up in hospital.

Taylor was shocked. He'd had no idea about all Paul's problems when he'd signed him! The manager could have easily washed his hands of Paul, especially when the team started doing well without him. But Taylor was a good man and vowed to help Paul get back on his feet.

When Paul started to feel better, he began training on his own. After each session, he would stop by the boss's office, where Taylor would always lend a friendly ear. Slowly but surely, Paul opened up to Taylor. He told him all about his tough start in life, growing up in orphanages and the bullying that came with it. It quickly became clear to Taylor that Ferguson at Manchester United hadn't got to know Paul at all. Paul wasn't a troublemaker – he had simply led a troubled life.

CHAPTER 14

THE VILLANS' VOTE

In the weeks and months that followed, Taylor proved to be the father figure Paul didn't know he needed.

'If things ever get bad again, you can come and stay with me and my wife,' Taylor offered.

That meant the world to Paul.

Villa's physio, Jim Walker, was another man who looked out for Paul. He could see that Paul's knee problems were adding to his pain, and he made a special training plan for the defender. Instead of running himself into the ground with the other lads, Paul would keep fit by training on a bike or doing weights for half an hour each day.

Some of the other players may have grumbled, but they soon stopped when they saw the sort of performances that Paul put in after that. Forming a strong back three with Derek Mountfield and Kent Nielsen, Paul quickly became Villa's best player!

The way Paul played the game had the fans on their feet. He never just hoofed the ball away or threw his body in front of it. His standard of defending was next level, and every touch he made was a clever chip or a brave backheel. He was such an elegant player!

Before long, a few of the fans began wearing shirts with 'GOD' printed above Paul's Number 5 on the back. It was a nickname that stuck!

With Taylor trusting in 'God', Villa began their march up the table. The previous season had seen them sucked into a relegation battle. Now they were fighting Liverpool for top spot. Incredible!

On Boxing Day 1989, Manchester United came to Villa Park. Since Paul (and Norman) had left the club, United were drifting dangerously close to the relegation zone themselves, with many fans calling for Ferguson to go.

In front of a crowd of 41,000 fans, Paul set about showing Ferguson why he had been so wrong to force him out, marshalling the defence as though his life depended on it.

'That's a positive first tackle from Paul McGrath,' the commentator raved.

Half-time arrived with Manchester United just about hanging on, only for Villa to take the lead in the fifty-sixth minute. After Gordon Cowan's free kick was only half-cleared, headers from Derek and then Paul tested United keeper Jim Leighton. Leighton couldn't save the ball a third time, though. He could only watch helplessly when Ian Olney slotted in the rebound from a narrow angle.

'Yesssss!' Paul punched the air.

Villa doubled their lead a few minutes later, when Ian set wing wizard Tony Daley down the right. Tony flew past his marker and squared the ball to David Platt, who danced around the keeper and finished with ease.

Manchester United had no reply. Instead, Villa sealed a perfect afternoon when Tony's magnificent cross was eventually drilled home by full-back Kevin Gage. That made it 3–0!

'What a load of rubbish!' the travelling Man United fans made their feelings clear.

'You're getting sacked in the morning!' the Villa fans in the Holte End joined in.

Ferguson trudged straight down the tunnel with his team, while the Villa players stayed out on the pitch, clapping their supporters long after the final whistle had blown.

Taylor put an arm around his Number 5. 'You were fantastic out there today, Paul! Facing your old club can't have been easy.'

By March, Villa were two points clear at the top. Paul and the defence were cruising to clean sheets, David Platt and Gordon Cowans were masters in midfield, and goal after goal was shared out among the team.

All was going well until a rumour began to bother the players. It was a badly kept secret that, at the end of the season, Taylor would be leaving the Villa to replace Bobby Robson as England boss.

Instead of focusing on the matches they had left to play, the players began worrying about who their next manager might be. Villa's results began to drop off, just as Liverpool were coming into the sort of form that had seen them crowned champions so many times that decade.

A defeat and two draws in Villa's last four matches of the season sadly weren't good enough to finish first, while Liverpool kept winning and winning and winning.

Still, Villa could be proud of how far they had come that season. They hadn't been in the title race for years. Second place was still a fantastic achievement!

Taylor's last match as Villa manager was a 3–3 draw away at Everton. It still wasn't official that he would be the new Three Lions boss, but all fans knew it was the end of an era.

When Paul said his own goodbyes to Taylor, it was hard to get the words out. Taylor deserved the England job, no doubt about it, but after everything they had been through together that past year, Paul was really going to miss him.

'You look after yourself, Paul,' said Taylor.

Paul promised he would try.

And despite the disappointments, there was a silver lining at the end of the season. The Villa fans had voted 'God' their Player of the Season!

Paul felt so grateful to call this club his new home.

CHAPTER 15

AN ITALIAN ADVENTURE

With a very busy season wrapped up, now wasn't the time to rest – not when there was a World Cup to be played! Ireland's green army of fans was delighted when their team managed a feat they never had before: they qualified for the biggest football tournament in the world. It had only taken thirteen attempts!

Two years on from the Euros, Ireland would again have to play England and the Netherlands, in a group with Egypt. No one really gave the Irish much of a chance of going far in the competition, but Charlton and the lads were determined to enjoy their Italian adventure.

Ireland's match with familiar foes England was a stormy encounter, not so much on the pitch as in the stadium itself!

England were out for revenge. Two years earlier, Ray and Pat had inspired a famous win that England hadn't forgotten. This time, as the wind swirled around the stadium in Sardinia, England opened the scoring early on. A scruffy Gary Lineker goal went in after only seven minutes.

In midfield, Paul led the fightback, directing a powerful header on goal that Peter Shilton had to scramble to save. Close! Ireland went into the break looking like the better side, but with nothing to show for all their hard work.

'Let's keep this up, lads!' said captain Mick McCarthy.

Rain began to lash down in the second half, but Ireland kept battling. The weather didn't bother Paul, who let fly from outside the box, only to see his shot fly over Shilton's goal.

With thunder and lightning threatening to end the game early, Ireland's chances of a point seemed all but lost. Kevin Sheedy had other ideas, though. The Everton man made the most of a mix-up at the back with a late strike to level the match. 1–1!

Ireland's next game was far less thrilling. Egypt used every trick in the book to waste time. The Pharaohs made boring backpass after boring backpass to their goalkeeper who happily hogged the ball. But instead of trying to get the ball down and play, Charlton seemed happy for his team to go for the draw. Ireland even began copying Egypt's tactics! It ended as an uneventful 0–0.

On the bench, Ireland's young striker, Niall Quinn, couldn't understand Charlton's tactics. 'We should have tried harder to score!' he moaned.

Now, to be sure of going through to the knockouts, Ireland had to either win or draw at the very least, against European champions the Netherlands. The whole team were kicking themselves!

Sadly in Sicily, Ireland made a sloppy start against the Dutch, allowing Ruud Gullit to slide home after a clever one-two with Wim Kieft . . . that man again!

Ireland went after the equaliser, harrying the Dutch defence, but without really testing their keeper Hans van Breukelen.

Then, just after the seventieth minute, Ireland's fortunes swung at last, with a goal that was textbook Charlton. Pat booted another hopeful high ball for one of Ireland's six-footers to try to nod down. A Dutch defender hit a bobbling ball back to his keeper, who spilled it in front of Niall's outstretched right boot.

Paul burst into the box, but Niall didn't need him. The substitute struck the ball cleanly past van Breukelen!

'Yesssssssssss!' Paul ran over to celebrate with Niall.

And that's how the match ended. Yet another draw, but the right result for Ireland!

England topped the group, with Ireland and the Netherlands second and third on the exact same goal difference. It would go to a lottery to decide their next opponents.

This time, the luck was with the Irish . . . the Boys in Green were drawn against Romania while the Netherlands faced the formidable West Germany!

On paper, there was not much to choose between Ireland and Romania – both teams had a 'golden generation' of players to choose from. Romania's playmaker was Gheorghe Hagi, whose first touch and dribbling skills would have the Irish defence on high alert.

Ninety minutes later in Genoa, neither side had managed to score. So on to extra time it was, with both teams mindful that one goal might win it.

Ireland were just about standing firm when Paul committed a foul on Lupu. Yellow card! Then, with frustration building, Paul clashed with Hagi towards the close of extra time. Irish fans held their breath as they waited for the ref's decision. Another booking would see Paul leave the pitch! Thankfully, the ref's red card stayed in his pocket and he told the players to get on with the match. Paul had learned his lesson.

Penalties beckoned. Pat was feeling confident, and so were Ireland's penalty-takers. Up stepped:

Sheedy ✓
Houghton ✓
Townsend ✓
And Cascarino ✓

That made it four out of four!

Romania, though, hadn't missed either. But when Daniel Timofte stepped up to take Romania's final spot-kick, Pat got a huge glove on the ball and pushed it away to safety. What a save! The keeper leapt for joy.

David O'Leary decided he was the man to carry the hopes of a nation into the next round. A classy centre-half, David was back in Ireland's squad after three years of being dropped. A nation held its breath, but there wasn't a flicker of doubt in David's mind . . . he slammed the ball past Lung.

5–4! Ireland were through to the World Cup quarter-finals!

Charlton jogged across to shake David's hand, but the defender was buried under a pile of green bodies. The players couldn't believe it! They all hugged, let go, and hugged again.

'If I live to be a hundred, I don't think I'll forget what I've just seen out there!' Charlton wiped away a tear.

Then Ireland marched on to Rome, where they would also visit the Vatican to meet the Pope!

CHAPTER 16

ALL ROADS LEAD TO ROME

'Can you believe we're actually here?' Kevin Moran asked Paul excitedly.

Paul opened his eyes and blinked, as the team bus pulled up outside Rome's famous Olympic Stadium. 'Wow! This place looks even bigger than Old Trafford.'

'It is!' Kevin replied. 'And next Sunday we could be back here for the final! Now wouldn't that be something!'

Paul smiled. It didn't hurt to dream. In fact, the whole tournament had felt like one long dream so far. He kept expecting to wake up any second.

By now, some huge teams had been knocked out of the competition. The Netherlands had been beaten,

Brazil and Spain too. Somehow, though, Ireland were still alive and kicking, one of only eight teams still in the chase for World Cup glory. Now they faced the host nation, Italy, the team of Franco Baresi and Roberto Baggio. Eek!

For their quarter-final, Charlton decided to switch formations and go 4–4–2, with Paul moving up from defence to anchor the midfield.

From the first whistle, both Ireland and Italy tried to move the ball around, creating plenty of chances. Before long, Ireland were playing their best football of the tournament . . . a thousand times better than in that dreadful draw with Egypt!

They almost went ahead after twenty-five minutes, when a header from Niall brought a flying save from Zenga. The chance had 15,000 Ireland fans inside the stadium on their feet! Close!

After that, Italy decided to take the game by the scruff of its neck. Donadoni fired at goal, but Pat could only paw the ball into the path of Italy hitman Salvatore 'Toto' Schillaci. Paul lunged desperately towards the ball but arrived a fraction of a second too late – Schillaci's powerful shot nestled just inside the far post, for 1–0.

The Italians in the crowd tried to start a Mexican wave next, which fell flat when the glum green shirts stayed glued to their seats. It was only on the fourth attempt that the Irish fans joined in the party, and the whole stadium erupted into cheers.

Who knows, thought the Ireland fans. *It might be exactly the lift our team needs!*

Early in the second half, Schillaci won his side a free kick on the edge of the box. When a teammate quickly tapped back to him, Schillaci unleashed a screamer that cannoned off the underside of the crossbar, onto the goal line, and back into play!

'Gooooaaaallll!' Schillaci appealed hopefully.

The ref shook his head. The whole of the ball had not crossed the line!

'No way it did!' Paul agreed.

With time running out, Charlton decided it was time for fresh legs. A striker for a striker, Tony Cascarino for Niall. The next Irish attempt, though, came from Paul, a fierce shot that stung Zenga's white glove.

'Ooh aah, Paul McGrath! Ooh aah, Paul McGrath!' came the chants from the Ireland fans.

'Come on, we're still in this!' Paul rallied his team.

Desperate to keep their fairy-tale alive, Ireland pushed on in search of an equaliser. They thought it was all over when Schillaci broke away and fired home, but the ref raised his arm to signal offside. And so the match ended 1–0, the narrow win taking Italy into the semis.

Ireland's dream may have been over, but their supporters were still smiling and clapping and waving their flags. There was no shame in going out to a strong Italian side, and to a single goal at that.

'Toto' Schillaci, meanwhile, went on to claim the Golden Boot and the Golden Ball for the tournament's top scorer and best player.

Later that year, there was a trophy for Paul too, when he was voted Ireland's Player of the Year. No matter where Charlton had asked him to play, Paul had been outstanding all year. He had been a quiet leader in a team that had given the fans in Italy and at home in Ireland such hope and joy. Their first World Cup had been so much more than a sporting tournament – it had brought a nation together.

CHAPTER 17

DIFFICULT DAYS

Following Graham Taylor's departure from Villa Park, a little-known manager called Jozef Vengloš from Czechoslovakia came in next. Vengloš was the first man born outside Great Britain and Ireland to manage in England's top flight.

Dr Jo, as he became known, was a sports scientist. He had lots of smart ideas about how to improve the team . . . through diet and nutrition and positive mindsets, which left the Aston Villa players scratching their heads. English football at the beginning of the nineties just wasn't ready for such modern thinking!

By Christmas, Villa had only managed four wins, all against struggling teams.

Away from the pitch, Paul was finding things tough too. Dark clouds were gathering over him that wouldn't blow away. The bond he had built with Graham Taylor wasn't there with Dr Jo, leaving Paul feeling more alone than ever.

Sadly, Paul's mental health suffered, and he found himself back in hospital. At first, he felt scared, but the doctors there helped him to focus on the things he loved the most: his family, playing football and the fans. Before long, Paul was well enough to go home.

'Paul McGrath? He doesn't look ill,' the fans might have said if they saw him on the pitch, but that was because he hid it so well. It was something he had been doing his whole life.

So, Paul did the only thing he knew would save him, and got back on the grass almost straight away.

While Taylor had taken Villa to the dizzy heights of second in Division One the season before, Villa nosedived to finish seventeenth under Vengloš. Sadly, he had to go.

Losing your boss was never fun, but when the club replaced him with Ron Atkinson, Paul smiled for the first time in a long time. Reunited with Big Ron! Their early days at Manchester United together had given Paul some of his happiest memories in football.

But when Atkinson arrived at Villa, he heard a lot of stories about Paul that he didn't want to believe were true. At United, Atkinson knew that Paul and the other young lads loved staying out late in town, but they always turned up for training on time and gave 100 per cent in matches. Since then, it seemed that Paul's problems off the pitch had become much more serious.

In Atkinson's first weeks as Villa boss, Paul thought he could take his foot off the gas, skipping pre-season training at Bodymoor Heath. Some days, he couldn't get out of bed after partying the night before.

'Ron will never drop me,' Paul convinced himself.

Behind the scenes, Atkinson was wondering whether it was time that Paul moved on. 'He would be someone else's problem then!' Atkinson told the club chairman.

Ireland legend Liam Brady was now the boss of Celtic. He was interested in taking Paul to Scotland, but only offered half the £1.5 million fee that might tempt Villa into selling.

It wasn't until Paul finally pulled his socks up on Villa's pre-season tour to Germany that his name was taken off the transfer list.

Dynamo Dresden were a strong and physical team, standing head and shoulders above some of the Villa players. Even Paul's opponent towered over the big defender.

No bother! thought Paul, while the players took up their positions on the pitch.

In the first minute, Dresden's centre-forward set off on a sprint. Paul set off too, steaming past his opponent to pick up the ball and – *ping!* – knock it away to safety.

Next came a corner. The two rose for a header together. *Bang!* Paul jumped half a foot higher to clear the ball up the field.

Atkinson's jaw dropped. Paul was a class apart!

'We can't sell our best player!' Atkinson rushed to tell the chairman back in Birmingham. 'It's as simple as that.'

So Paul was allowed to stay, on the understanding that any more missed training sessions or bad behaviour would see his wages docked.

During that season with Atkinson at the helm, Villa shot back up the table to finish in seventh place. Much more like it!

The season after that, the first of the shiny new Premier League era, Atkinson strengthened his squad with a couple of new signings: Paul's Republic of Ireland teammate Ray Houghton, a tireless midfielder, and the Welsh striker Dean Saunders from Liverpool, who would share the goal-scoring with Dwight Yorke and Dalian Atkinson.

All plans to let Paul leave had been forgotten. The defender was in his thirties now, but there was no chance Atkinson was selling him – Paul was priceless on the pitch!

Manchester United and Aston Villa were neck and neck in the title race until April, when the two teams were dealt different cards. While Atkinson's Villa squad was hit with some unfortunate injuries, Manchester United kept racking up the points by scoring deep into added time.

'Referees won't blow their whistles until United have scored the winner!' the fans of other teams complained.

'That's just sour grapes!' the United fans replied.

It began to happen so often, though, that added time at Old Trafford became known as 'Fergie Time'. In the end, Manchester United won the very first Premier League by ten points, but there was a trophy for Paul too: the other Premier League players had voted him their Player of the Year!

Despite so many difficult days off the pitch, Paul was at the top of his game on it. After years of keeping the best strikers quiet, his talents were being rewarded. It was a proud moment when he collected the enormous trophy at a fancy London hotel. The only Irish player to win the award before Paul had been his hero Liam Brady. It felt like a fairy-tale to follow in such famed footsteps!

CHAPTER 18

PREPARING FOR BATTLE

The League Cup final in 1994 offered Aston Villa the chance for revenge. Their semi-final had seen them scrape through a penalty shoot-out with Tranmere Rovers for the chance to play . . . Manchester United!

Any time Villa faced his old club, Paul never needed any extra motivation. He always raised his game, desperate to show Alex Ferguson he'd made a major mistake by getting rid of him.

On the morning of the final, though, Paul wasn't sure if he could play at all. For a while now, the Villa star had been carrying an injury that suddenly seemed to feel worse.

Over breakfast at the team hotel, he was feeling very sorry for himself. He hadn't had a wink's sleep the whole night – hardly the best preparation for a cup final.

'You look awful, Paul,' said Atkinson, who had seen him looking worse for wear on plenty of occasions.

'It's my neck,' Paul moaned, turning his head slowly to one side.

'Get this down you,' Atkinson held out a cup of hot coffee. 'Then go see the physio.'

To numb the pain, the club physio Jim decided to give Paul an injection in his shoulder. It wasn't a treatment to be taken lightly. Jim explained there might be side effects and once the injection wore off, the pain would hit worse than before. But if Paul wanted to play, it was the only option.

Manchester United had power in every position, except for possibly one: their goalkeeper, Peter Schmeichel was suspended! There was no doubt that Villa were still the underdogs, but without the Great Dane in goal, the Villa strikers would fancy their chances.

Five minutes before the game, Paul was kitted up and ready to go, when the pain started shooting back through his shoulder. Would Villa have to make a change to their line-up too?

Jim was in the middle of giving Paul another injection when the buzzer for the players to take the field suddenly sounded. Poor Paul leapt out of his seat!

'You don't have to play, you know,' said Ray, worried about his friend.

Paul swatted away his concern like a bothersome fly. 'I'll be grand in a minute or two.'

Of course Paul had to play – he had a starring role! The newspapers were calling the match 'The Battle of the Gods' . . . pitting Paul McGrath against Eric Cantona!

So, feeling a little dazed, Paul joined his team in the tunnel. Behind him was Ferguson, shaking hands with Atkinson. Paul turned away. Since leaving United, he and Fergie hadn't exchanged a single word.

While Paul took his place at the heart of the Aston Villa defence, the Villa fans were already singing loudly. That soon cheered him up!

The fans would be delighted if their team somehow pulled off a result – Villa hadn't lifted a trophy since their famous European Cup victory in 1982!

Villa came quickly out of the blocks, while Manchester United's speed of passing was surprisingly slow. And when Dalian gave Villa a shock lead, their players began to believe that the match would only go one way. It was a great goal, a clever flick from Dean over the United defence into Dalian's path to score. *Lovely!*

On seventy minutes, Villa scored again, this time when Dean diverted Kevin Richardson's free kick past the United keeper. Mark Hughes pulled a goal back for Man United soon after, but Villa kept fighting until the final whistle. Next, a super strike from Tony Daley hit the post, but fell kindly to Dalian. Dalian let fly but saw his shot saved on the line by the hand of Manchester United winger Andrei Kanchelskis.

The handball didn't look deliberate, but the ref gave the penalty anyway and showed Kanchelskis a red card. *Unlucky!*

Deano was delighted to score his second of

the game. 3–1!

Paul felt dizzy with delight too, a combination of the injections and the knowledge that in the Battle of the Gods, he had definitely come out on top.

The TV cameras interviewed Atkinson and Paul together. 'Well done on your victory today,' the presenter congratulated them. 'Ron, how do you think Paul handled Eric Cantona today?'

'Cantona? Are you sure he was playing?' Atkinson joked. He couldn't remember the fiery Frenchman having a kick!

Paul gave a humble smile and handed the mic back as fast as he could. He was about to head down the tunnel when:

'Well done, big man,' came a voice from behind him.

Paul turned around. It was Alex Ferguson, offering an outstretched hand. There were no hard feelings, it appeared, at least on Fergie's part.

Paul was gobsmacked. 'Th–thank you, Alex,' he managed to blurt out.

In that moment, the hurt from his Man United exit

suddenly stung a little less. This wasn't a time to look back – Paul had just won his first trophy with Villa and it was time to celebrate!

Back in Birmingham, Paul's painful shoulder felt worse than ever. The club contacted the best doctors to see what treatment to give their star man. It turned out that the shoulder pain was caused by a virus, and there was no quick fix.

'It will most likely take six months to recover properly,' one doctor explained.

'But the World Cup is *three* months away!' Paul moaned.

It would be a battle against time to be fit enough to travel to the United States.

Paul was prepared to do anything to make Ireland's World Cup squad. He sat out the next half-dozen games to rest his injury, until at last, the pain levels had dropped from agonising to just about bearable. But with the season drawing to an end, Paul needed some match practice. He begged to be selected for Villa's game against Southampton.

Sadly, the comeback came too soon. A passenger on

the pitch at the Dell, Paul just couldn't move freely. In the end, he called to the bench to be brought off as Villa went down 4–1. *Noooooooo!*

A determined Paul tried again, in Villa's final home match against Liverpool. This time, he found a way to play through the pain and managed much better. Dwight's double in the second half sent the fans home happy.

Now to rest properly, thought Paul. Exactly one month remained until Ireland were due to fly out to America for the World Cup.

CHAPTER 19

WORLD CLASS

Of course Paul made Ireland's World Cup squad for USA '94 – was it ever in doubt? Charlton believed even a half-fit Paul would win him matches.

'We could never leave you behind,' Charlton told his trusted defender.

Paul was counting his lucky stars on the flight to Florida. There was no better feeling than pulling on an Ireland shirt at a big tournament, especially when his new wife Caroline and their boys would be in the crowd to see him play.

The plane landed on the tarmac at Orlando Airport to temperatures twice as hot as the squad were used to playing in. The next ten days of training there were set to be tough. New Jersey, where Ireland were due to play Italy, wouldn't be much cooler either.

Ireland had never beaten Italy, who were always among the favourites when it came to the top tournaments. Paul thought back to when the teams had last met at the 1990 World Cup. That day Italy, the host nation, had come out on top, scoring a single goal that had sent Ireland crashing out of the competition in the quarter-finals. The luck of the Irish had gone missing in action in Rome.

Four years on in New Jersey, some of the same names from that night again appeared in Italy and Ireland's starting elevens. Italy had the rock-solid Franco Baresi and Paolo Maldini at the back, with the pony-tailed Roberto Baggio leading the line once more. Charlton considered Baggio to be Italy's biggest dangerman, and gave Paul the job of marking him.

It felt amazing when Paul looked around the Giants Stadium – the colour green seemed to have flooded into every stand. Fans who had travelled for the tournament, plus plenty more Irish who now called the United States home.

Paul passed his first test after eight minutes, when Baggio put Signori through on goal. Now Paul was in a foot-race to see who could reach the ball first. With his damaged shoulder causing the arm to hang limp by his side, Paul put on a burst of speed to arrive just ahead of Signori and nick the ball back to Pat. What an interception!

A goal from Ray did wonders to settle Irish nerves soon after. When Ray spotted the Italian goalkeeper off his line, he launched a left-footed strike from outside the box. The goal sailed over the head of Gianluca Pagliuca and was followed by a somersaulting celebration!

Italy pushed forwards in search of an equaliser, but couldn't find a way past Paul, who was like a one-man wall. After making a triple block, Paul wiped his brow with the sweatband on his wrist. By now, his shoulder was throbbing – half-time couldn't come soon enough!

In the changing room, the players stripped off their sweat-soaked shirts and lay flat on their backs on the cool concrete floor.

'We've got them on the run!' Charlton told

his players.

The coach was right – Italy were rattled. If Ireland could keep up their brilliant defensive display in the second half, three World Cup points would be theirs!

Italy shuffled their side at the break, swapping strikers, Daniele Massaro for Guiseppe Signori. But young Phil Babb and Paul teamed up together tremendously at the back, shutting down attack after attack until the final whistle brought Irish relief at last.

History had been made! Ireland had beaten Italy! Fans in their thousands danced in New Jersey and in Dublin!

Paul allowed himself a smile. That had to be up there with one of the best performances of his career. The big defender had just proved to the millions of people watching that he was world class. What a day! And it wasn't over yet . . .

There waiting outside the Irish changing room was Franco Baresi.

'Paul McGrath . . . the best defender I ever saw play!' Baresi said.

Me? thought Paul. *He can't be serious!*

But Baresi wasn't messing around. He took off his shirt and offered it to Paul, expecting Paul's in return.

Then Paul smiled and made the swap. It would be one to show the grandkids!

The next match for the Boys in Green was back in sweltering Orlando, with their opponents Mexico much more at ease playing in the heat. After losing their first match in Group E, Mexico needed some points of their own.

Sadly, Ireland's performance against Mexico lacked the magic of the Italy game. A Luis García double gave Mexico a two-goal lead, with substitute John Aldridge the only Irish player able to find the back of the net. While Ireland couldn't salvage a point, every World Cup goal was to be celebrated.

Ireland went into their third and final group game with Norway under pressure. They would need at least a point to go through to the knockouts.

'If you get the ball, knock it long,' Charlton urged his defenders.

Not everyone agreed with the boss's boring tactics,

they had some decent midfielders who were more than capable of keeping possession: Ray, Roy Keane, John Sheridan – they all wanted to be on the ball.

That day, the Irish forwards weren't firing. Luckily, neither were Norway. The match ended a 0–0 draw. Was it enough to stay in the competition? Just about!

All the teams in Group E had four points, but only Mexico, Ireland and Italy made the next round. Norway were bowing out having scored fewer goals. Agony!

It would be back to the Citrus Bowl Stadium in Orlando for Ireland's Round of 16 game. The good news was that their European opponents wouldn't like the heat any more than the Irish team. The bad news? They were drawn against the Netherlands. Not again! The Ireland fans were still getting over the dodgy Dutch goal that had denied their team a famous win at the last World Cup!

CHAPTER 20

KNOCKED OUT

The Netherlands' experience of the 1994 World Cup so far had been far nervier than they had liked. Despite their squad including quality players like Dennis Bergkamp, Ronald Koeman and the de Boer twins, they had been minutes away from an early exit in Orlando. In the end the Dutch were saved by Bryan Roy's late winner in their final game against Morocco. That single goal suddenly catapulted the Netherlands team to the top of Group F on goal difference.

Ireland were dreaming of going further into the competition but were happy to be the underdogs against the mighty Netherlands. No one was too surprised when the Dutch took an early lead with just over ten minutes gone. Tricky winger Marc Overmars set it up, crossing to the menacing Dennis Bergkamp. Bergkamp reached the ball a split second ahead of Paul and slid home past Irish keeper Pat Bonner. So annoying!

The Dutch defence, meanwhile, were standing firm, limiting Ireland to long-range shots. But when Wim Jonk tried his luck from a distance, Pat was caught completely off-guard. Ireland's keeper let the shot slip through his gloves for 2–0! Jonk couldn't believe his luck.

'Don't worry about it, Pat,' said Paul, trying to console his keeper, but there was no escaping the fact it was a costly mistake.

In the second half, the Dutch drew deeper in a bid to protect their lead. It wasn't until four minutes from time that Ireland had their first real chance of the game. Substitute Tony Cascarino found Phil unmarked in the box, but the defender's shot flashed inches wide.

Then came a chance for Ireland's other centre-half. With the orange section of the crowd whistling for the ref to blow, Paul stretched his leg high to bring down a lofty pass from Ray. Beautifully done, he fired the ball past the Dutch keeper Ed de Goey and into the back of the net.

Gooooooaaaaallllll!

Or so Paul thought. The next moment, though, the strike was ruled out for dangerous play. Dutch defender Frank Rijkaard, still holding his head, had convinced the ref he'd been struck by Paul's boot during the build-up.

'He's faked that, for sure!' said an outraged Ray.

'Fair play,' Paul replied. He would probably have done the same thing if it had been at the other end of the pitch.

What a shame! Had the goal stood, it still wouldn't have been enough to take Ireland through, but it would certainly have been one of Paul's best strikes in a green shirt.

Seconds later, it was time to shake hands. There were no hard feelings between Paul and Frank Rijkaard. The Dutch had been the better side, and they deserved to go through.

The Boys in Green stayed on the pitch until they had

clapped every emerald shirt in the ground. Ireland hadn't
The Boys in Green stayed on the pitch until they had
clapped every emerald shirt in the ground. Ireland hadn't
conjured too many magical moments over the past four
matches, but the fans kept on cheering all the same.

'Ooh aah, Paul McGrath! Ooh aah, Paul McGrath!'
Paul never got bored of hearing that one!

The team landed back at Dublin Airport to a
heroes' welcome. The excitement levels were even
higher than when they had come home from Italy
four years earlier! The celebrations continued at
Phoenix Park, where 100,000 people gathered to
show their appreciation. It wasn't just Ireland's usual
male fans – there were women, children, even some
babies in their prams.

'What other nation's fans would show up like this
to support a team that only had one World Cup win to
their name?' Paul couldn't help but wonder.

'We've got the best fans in the world!' his Ireland
and Villa teammate, Andy Townsend added.

Paul looked out at all the smiling faces, trying to
soak it all in. A moment like this might never come

again. With the injuries that had bothered him for years now, it would take a miracle to still be playing when the next World Cup rolled around.

'I'll be thirty-eight by then,' he realised.

Andy's face fell. He knew the day would inevitably arrive when Paul would play his last match in a green shirt, but he didn't want to think about it. 'Get away with you, Macca! You'll outlast us all!'

Ireland would of course have to qualify for the tournament first, a tough task in itself. Paul wasn't the only player of Ireland's golden generation likely to hang up his boots before then, and Charlton's reign as boss would one day come to an end too.

Those thoughts were for another day, though. First it was time to party!

CHAPTER 21

A THIRD TROPHY

Back at Aston Villa, a new season began. Villa made a fair start, going unbeaten in their first five league matches, before their form suddenly fell off a cliff. Over the nine games that followed, Villa managed just one point. Not surprisingly, they found themselves in the relegation zone. What a woeful run!

Then came a bombshell straight out of the claret and blue! The club had parted ways with its manager Ron Atkinson.

Shockwaves crashed around the changing room. Yes, results had been bad, but none of the players had seen this coming. They would have done anything for the gaffer. Just seven months earlier,

Atkinson had masterminded that famous victory over Manchester United at Wembley to bag the club's first trophy in years.

'He didn't deserve the sack!' Paul complained at Bodymoor Heath, and all his teammates agreed.

Paul was really going to miss the big man, but more than that, he was worried about keeping his place in the side. There were no guarantees that whoever came in next would be so kind to him . . . putting up with Paul doing almost zero training and letting him fly home to Ireland whenever he was feeling low.

Atkinson's replacement, who arrived a couple of weeks later, turned out to be a familiar face at the club. Brian Little had once entertained the Holte End as Villa's star striker, and had since stepped into management.

By January, a clutch of players Little considered to be past their best, including Paul's Irish teammate Ray Houghton, were moved on to other clubs. Paul breathed a sigh of relief to find he wouldn't be joining them.

Little's side didn't set Villa Park alight that season, but they did beat the drop. An eighteenth-place finish was just enough to keep them up in the Premiership, as four clubs below them were doomed to Division One. In the end, Paul made more appearances than anyone at Villa.

In the summer of 1995, Brian decided to freshen up his squad, splashing the cash on Gareth Southgate for a record £2.5 million, before forward Savo Milošević smashed the club record again soon after, costing a cool £3.5 million. Now came the test: how would the new boys gel with the rest of the team?

Little's decision to switch Gareth from midfield to central defence turned out to be his best tactic yet as Villa manager. A back three made up of Paul, Gareth and Ugo Ehiogu saw Villa form a mean defence that season, keeping plenty of clean sheets. Paul went into every match feeling ten feet tall – no striker could get past the mighty Macca!

Further up the field, meanwhile, Dwight and the new boy Savo were scoring freely. Under Brian Little, football felt fun again! The Villa players were much happier competing at the top of the table; last year's relegation battle seemed a distant bad dream now. And it wasn't just in the league where Villa were hitting top form – they were firing in both cups too.

Two years on from their League Cup triumph over Manchester United, Villa found themselves back at Wembley to try to win back the trophy, this time against a decent Leeds United side.

Ahead of the warm-up, some of the younger players looked nervous. Paul tried to set their minds at ease. 'We'll be grand, don't worry,' he promised. 'Just go out and enjoy it, it's not every day you get to play at Wembley.'

The Villa defender already knew that his job was to mark Tony Yeboah, Leeds's goal-hungry Ghanaian striker, yet still he didn't feel flustered.

'He can only fire up that rocket of a right foot if we give him space,' Paul told Gareth and Ugo. 'And we're not about to let that happen.'

'Definitely not!' they agreed.

The match got underway with the Villa fans loud and proud from the start. The Leeds goalkeeper John Lukic did well to block a shot from Dwight early on, but there was nothing he could do to keep out Villa next. When Savo charged towards goal, his marker foolishly backed off. The Villa man wasn't about to shoot from that far out, was he? Yes, he was! *Goooooaaaaalllll!*

'What an absolute belter!' Paul could barely believe his eyes.

Goals for Ian Taylor and Dwight followed in the second half, with Leeds unable to offer anything in reply. Tony Yeboah barely had a kick all game. Before long, Paul was proved right – Villa had won the cup at a canter! It was a victory that matched Liverpool's record – both teams had now won the cup five times.

Fireworks fizzed and flags waved as the Villa players and staff climbed the Wembley steps to claim back their trophy. Of course, the fans saved one of their loudest cheers for when 'God' held the trophy aloft!

Thirty-six years old and still winning silverware, life for Paul was pretty special!

A week later, Villa missed out on a second Wembley final when they slumped to a 3–0 defeat to Liverpool in their FA Cup semi-final. As the end of a hard season beckoned, Little's side was fast running out of steam.

The title run-in was a two-horse race between the Uniteds of Manchester and Newcastle, with Ferguson masterminding the Red Devils' third title in four seasons. Behind them were Liverpool, while Little guided Villa to a fine fourth place.

Paul felt proud of how far the team had come in twelve months. Not only had they won a trophy, but finishing fourth had earned them European football next season. Who knew where Villa might travel to compete in the UEFA Cup . . . Milan, Monaco, Munich even? Exciting times lay ahead.

CHAPTER 22

DERBY DEBUT

Paul knew that to compete against the best players in England and beyond, he would have to earn his place in a much-improved Villa side. With every season that passed, the game seemed to be getting faster, more physical. So far, Paul was keeping up, but he understood his playing days were numbered.

So that summer, Paul picked up the pace, doing sit-ups, press-ups, completing cross-country runs, eating healthily and drinking only water. When the players reported back at Bodymoor for pre-season training, Paul felt fitter than he had in years. He was ready for whatever the season could throw at him, except for what happened next . . .

Sheffield Wednesday were Villa's first opponents in the league. Paul always loved playing at Hillsborough and so was disappointed to discover that he had only made the bench. Wednesday ran out 2–1 winners, with no minutes on the pitch for Paul. But Villa bounced back to win the next three games without conceding a goal, while Paul didn't play a single second. Of course, it wasn't the first time Paul had been dropped in his career, but missing matches when he was in such good shape felt like a body blow.

Paul needed answers, so he went to speak to the manager. Little was businesslike and honest when he explained his plans for the season ahead. Villa would play a 4–4–2 formation: Gareth and Ugo would be the starting centre-backs, with Steve Staunton as their back-up.

A lesser player might have been happy to keep the bench warm and quietly retire at the end of the season. But not Paul!

'I can't just sit on the bench . . . I've got to play!' he pleaded.

Sadly, Little had other ideas. So after seven sensational seasons, Paul put in for a transfer and Villa agreed to let him go. So much for playing in Europe.

Derby County were a team that had just been promoted to the Premier League after five years in the second tier. So far, they had begun the season brightly and were already into double figures for points. Manager Jim Smith had put together a young squad with plenty of ambition but needed to add one or two experienced players to avoid going straight back down.

So when Paul became available, one of the league's most dependable defenders, Smith snapped him up straightaway. If anyone could keep Derby in the top flight, it was a player nicknamed 'God'!

Paul arrived at Derby's training ground one October morning in 1996, twenty-four hours before the Rams were due to face high-fliers Newcastle United at the Baseball Ground. When some of the club's young players saw Paul turn up on the training pitch in a Derby tracksuit, they couldn't believe their luck. With Paul in the team, anything was possible!

Derby's assistant coach Steve McClaren led training, while Smith watched over the session from his office. Paul set about training exactly as he had at Villa, a couple of leisurely laps around the pitch on his own, before heading back inside for a massage from the physios. On his way, he passed the boss's office.

'Paul, why aren't you training?' Smith looked angry.

'Boss, I don't train on Thursdays and Fridays,' Paul explained. 'I just play on Saturday.'

So that's how a thirty-six-year-old with two dodgy knees could get through ninety minutes in the Premier League! But instead of blasting his new signing, all Smith said was, 'No problem, Paul.' If that's what had worked for Villa, it would have to do for Derby!

The very next day, Paul went straight into Derby's defence, with the job of man-marking the world's most expensive footballer, Newcastle's own new signing, Alan Shearer. Smith knew it was a risk; Paul hadn't played a Premiership game in months, and was up against the league's deadliest striker, but it was a risk the Derby boss was willing to take.

'Don't worry, gaffer, I'm ready,' Paul promised.

Ninety minutes later, Paul left the pitch as the Player of the Match. Apart from one moment when Shearer had managed to evade Paul's clutches and slip a shot past Derby's keeper, Paul had kept the striker in his pocket the whole game. He'd rolled back the years to deliver a defensive masterclass!

'That was incredible!' Derby defender Chris Powell told his new teammate.

'Not bad for my first game in a while, I guess,' Paul replied humbly.

With each month that passed, the boss grew more impressed with his signing. True, Paul would never win any best trainer awards, but when it came to playing matches, he made defending look effortless. And he somehow managed to make everyone around him up their game too.

That season, Smith picked Paul whenever the defender's troublesome knees would allow it. In turn, Paul helped Derby climb the table to finish a strong twelfth. The Rams even managed to beat champions Manchester United, with a wonder goal from Paolo Wanchope and an impeccable Paul shoring up the backline. Another Player of the Match trophy belonged to Paul. How many awards did that make now? He had never thought to keep count.

Halfway through the season, Paul played his final game for Ireland, a 0–0 draw with Wales. After Charlton had resigned the year before, the new manager Mick McCarthy wanted to give some younger players their chance. Paul respected McCarthy's decision, and they wished each other well. Growing up, Paul would have been delighted with three caps for his country. In the end, he won eighty-three.

Paul's stay at Derby was short but sweet, a single season in the end. The Premiership was a fast and furious league which took no prisoners.

When the season ended, he made the decision to drop down a division, to keep playing for as long as he could. Paul would forever be grateful to Smith and the Derby fans for welcoming him with open arms, but it made sense for him to make one last move . . . to Sheffield United.

CHAPTER 23

END OF AN ERA

In the weeks leading up to his thirty-eighth birthday, Paul began to realise that something was very wrong. After a busy run of matches at Sheffield United, he could still read the game as well as ever, but his feet would no longer do what his brain was telling them. Every time Paul received the ball, he kept giving it away again. *What was going on?* He felt like a robot that was slowly starting to malfunction. It was the beginning of the end.

When Sheffield United travelled to Ipswich Town in early November 1997, three important points were at stake. Both teams were pushing hard for promotion back to the Premier League.

'Go give these fans an early present,' manager Nigel Spackman told his team.

But try as he might, Paul just couldn't keep control of the ball, passing it straight to Ipswich's attackers over and over. Now his teammates were forced to step in and help.

'Wake up, Paul!' captain David Holdsworth boomed.

The next attack saw Paul panic and boot the ball into touch, with no opponent even close. It was a horrible feeling, Paul didn't want the team to have to carry him, but he could barely kick straight!

On the sidelines, the manager looked on, his arms folded.

Ipswich Town 2, Sheffield United 2. One point on the road.

Paul chose a seat by himself on the bus back to Yorkshire that night. He was pretending to doze so that no one would bother him when his wife Caroline called on his new mobile phone. 'What happened out there?' She sounded concerned.

Paul couldn't explain. It was a strange sensation. For the first time in his career, he felt powerless to help his team. It was time for an honest conversation with the coach.

A night of tossing and turning followed, as a hundred thoughts raced through Paul's head. It wasn't even halfway through the season. On one hand he felt guilty for letting his teammates down, but on the other he was taking up the spot of someone who could give their all in a Blades shirt. He wasn't sure his heart would ever be ready to give up the game for good, but the rest of his body was screaming that he was done.

The next morning, when the rest of the squad had finished training, Paul knocked on the manager's door. Sweat beaded on his forehead as he sat down opposite Nigel Spackman.

'Really sorry, boss, but I just can't carry on,' he blurted out.

Spackman knew what this was straight away . . . Paul's retirement speech. He paused for a moment. 'You one hundred per cent sure, Paul?' the boss asked. 'Your contract is until the end of the season, that's a lot of money to be giving up.'

Paul nodded sadly. It wasn't about the money. His whole career, it had never been about the money.

'I want the fans to remember me as I was,' he explained . . . the turbocharged MGB that had won trophies, not a Robin Reliant, fit only for the scrapheap. The thought was almost unbearable.

It was plain to Spackman that there was no point in trying to make Paul change his mind. Before him stood a player who had given every last drop of energy to football, and who had nothing left in the tank.

Paul stuck out his hand for the boss to shake, but instead Spackman pulled him in for a huge hug.

The gaffer's reaction took Paul by surprise, but found the hug was just what he needed.

'Once a Blade, always a Blade,' Spackman said kindly. 'You'll forever be welcome here.'

Paul smiled. That wasn't so bad, after all.

And although Paul had hung up his boots in England, his final minutes on a football pitch were yet to play out. At the end of the season, a special testimonial match to celebrate Paul's amazing football career was arranged in Dublin. It would give the Irish fans the opportunity to say a proper thank you to their hero – one last chance to bring out that famous *ooh-aah* chant!

So on a cloudy day in May 1998, more than 37,000 fans flooded into Lansdowne Road Stadium for Paul's grand farewell. A star-studded Republic of Ireland XI were taking on an International XI, made up of Paul's old teammates from his past clubs, including Man United and Aston Villa. The two teams were stacked with talent!

'Don't think I'm going to go easy on you,' Dwight Yorke warned his old teammate.

'Catch yourself on, Yorky,' Robbie Keane leapt to Paul's defence. 'You'll not get past our Macca!'

Alongside the players, a footballing great came back to manage the Boys in Green.

'Paul McGrath . . .' said Big Jack Charlton. 'Aren't you a sight for sore eyes!'

Paul smiled. 'That's the first time in my career you've got my name right . . . and most likely the last!'

With the crowding chanting his name, a tearful Paul entered the action late in the game. It was the most minutes his knees would let him play. The cheer that met his arrival on the pitch was as loud as any he could remember.

I'll miss this, thought Paul. Football had given him the best memories of his life.

He could never have imagined that decades later, he would still be remembered as one of the finest players ever to pull on an Ireland shirt. Paul would forever be 'God' in the fans' eyes.

Read on for a sneak preview of
another brilliant classic football hero . . .

KEANE

Available now!

CHAPTER 1

"WE'VE GOT OUR TROPHY BACK!"

11 May 2003, Goodison Park – Final Day of the Premier League Season

Roy Keane had seen it all during his Manchester United career, including his fair share of drama on the final day of the season.

Today was different, though. There was a relaxed mood as Roy and his teammates stepped off the team bus and walked towards the away dressing room at Goodison Park. United would be taking on Everton in a few hours, but the Premier League trophy was already theirs.

After a tense, thrilling title race, United had held off Arsenal with a game to spare. This afternoon's season finale had once looked like a must-win game, but now it would be more of a celebration.

'Over the years, we've won the title on the final day and lost the title on the final day,' said Roy's teammate Ryan Giggs, or 'Giggsy' as they all called him. 'I've got to admit, it's nice not to have that pressure this year.'

Roy grinned, thinking back over the ten years of games that he and Giggsy had played together. 'Yeah, and even after everything we've won, this feeling never gets old,' he replied.

This was Roy's seventh time as a Premier League champion. Like Giggsy, he had been part of the early glory years, playing alongside Eric Cantona, Bryan Robson and Steve Bruce – and he had kept United on top as the team got younger, with David Beckham and the rest of the club's famous academy group bursting on to the scene. Roy had been the engine powering the Treble-winning season in 1999, and four years on he was still leading the squad, with deadly Dutch striker Ruud van Nistelrooy joining an experienced core.

He didn't usually allow himself to dwell on all these achievements, but this latest title felt extra sweet.

The clock on the dressing room wall was ticking down towards kick-off, and when United manager Sir Alex Ferguson walked in, the noise quietened a little. Ferguson usually had that effect.

'I know you're all thinking about lifting the trophy again, and I am too,' Ferguson said. 'But let's finish it off in style, like proper champions do.'

Roy nodded. He hated to lose, and he knew he wouldn't enjoy the party later if United had a total no-show. Readjusting the captain's armband on his sleeve, he stood up and gulped down some water.

'Let's go, lads,' he said, heading for the tunnel.

The players walked out to a sea of blue around the stadium and a roar from the home fans, but this kind of atmosphere was nothing new for Roy or his teammates. Playing for Manchester United meant dealing with high pressure and high expectations – they were the team that everyone wanted to beat.

MCGRATH HONOURS

Manchester United
🏆 FA Cup winners 1984–85

Aston Villa
🏆 League Cup winners 1993–94, 1995–96

Individual
🏆 PFAI Players' Player of the Year, 1982
🏆 PFA Team of the Year, 1985–86 (First Division), 1992–93 (Premier League)
🏆 Aston Villa Player of the Season, 1989–90, 1990–91, 1991–92, 1992–93

- 🏆 FAI Senior International Player of the Year, 1990, 1991
- 🏆 PFA Players' Player of the Year, 1993
- 🏆 Football League 100 Legends, 1998
- 🏆 English Football Hall of Fame, 2015
- 🏆 FAI Hall of Fame, 2020

McGRATH

5 MCGRATH

NAME:
Paul McGrath

DATE OF BIRTH:
4 December 1959

PLACE OF BIRTH:
Greenford, England

NATIONALITY:
Irish

POSITION:
CD, DM

THE STATS

Height (cm):	185
Club appearances:	598
Club goals:	31
Club trophies:	3
International appearances:	83
International goals:	8
International trophies:	0
BALLON D'ORS:	0

★ ★ ★ **HERO RATING: 88** ★ ★ ★

GREATEST MOMENTS

5 FEBRUARY 1985, REPUBLIC OF IRELAND 1–2 ITALY

An injury to Mark Lawrenson saw manager Eoin Hand give Paul an unexpected debut for the Boys in Green in a friendly against Italy. Ireland may have lost the match at an electric Dalymount Park, but it was an experience that the young defender would never forget.

27 MARCH 1991, ENGLAND 1–1 REPUBLIC OF IRELAND

The old Wembley Stadium was the venue for Ireland's tricky Euros qualifier. The demand for tickets was so high, the ground could have sold out three times over. While the home side struck first, Paul claimed an important assist when he floated a ball into the box towards Niall Quinn, who slotted the ball past David Seaman for the equaliser.

27 MARCH 1994, ASTON VILLA 3–1 MANCHESTER UNITED

When Paul took on Eric Cantona in a 'Battle of the Gods', it was the Villa man who came out on top . . . was Cantona even playing? Paul got one over his old manager and denied Manchester United the treble to boot. Revenge was sweet!

18 JUNE 1994, ITALY 0–1 REPUBLIC OF IRELAND

It was at the 1994 World Cup where Paul put in one of the performances of his career. In the scorching New York sun and with two dodgy knees, Paul stopped striker Roberto Baggio from scoring, as Ireland claimed a famous win.

24 MARCH 1996, ASTON VILLA 3–0 LEEDS UNITED

Paul completed a hat-trick of trophies won at Wembley as opponents Leeds United fell apart. A clean sheet and three good goals handed Villa their fifth League Cup, a record held jointly with Liverpool at the time.

6. 17 MAY 1998, REPUBLIC OF IRELAND XI V INTERNATIONAL XI

More than 37,000 fans filled Lansdowne Road for Paul's testimonial, a match that saw him sign off from football for good. The teams were stacked with his closest teammates from club and country with Big Jack Charlton as Ireland's gaffer. Paul even managed to hobble a lap of honour for the fans!

TEST YOUR KNOWLEDGE

QUESTIONS

1. Which English club did Paul support while growing up?

2. Was Paul's junior football club called Pearse Athletic or Pearse Rovers?

3. What was the colour of the St Patrick's shirt that Paul wore?

4. Which Manchester United manager sold Paul to Aston Villa?

5. Which nation knocked Paul and the Ireland national team out of Euro 1988?

6. Who were the opposition when Paul won the FA Cup with Manchester United?

7. In which country did Paul and Ireland play their first World Cup?

8. Who did Paul swap shirts with after Ireland's famous World Cup win over Italy?

9. Which of Paul's clubs is nicknamed 'The Red Devils'?

10. At which club did Paul end his playing days?

Answers below . . . No cheating!

1. Chelsea. 2. Pearse Rovers. 3. Red. 4. Alex Ferguson. 5. Netherlands. 6. Everton. 7. Italy. 8. Franco Baresi. 9. Manchester United. 10. Sheffield United.

PLAY LIKE YOUR HEROES

WIN TACKLES LIKE PAUL MCGRATH

STEP 1: No matter where the action is on the pitch, you need to stay alert and read the game. Your opponents could launch a goal-scoring attack in an instant.

STEP 2: When the time comes to make a tackle, never dive straight in. First, scan the pitch quickly to see where the opposition's attacking players are positioned.

STEP 3: Timing is everything! Commit too early and the attacker could pass or dribble around you. Leaving it late is risky too, as the ball is likely to have been moved on, or you could give away a foul.

STEP 4: Get your body between your opponent and the goal to block their path. Make sure you are close enough to win the ball cleanly, then quickly decide what sort of tackle is needed. Should you stand firm and make a block tackle, or could you poke the ball away from the side?

STEP 5: After making the challenge, don't hang around on the ball. Look for any teammates in space, it could be your chance to launch a quick counterattack!

CAN'T GET ENOUGH OF
ULTIMATE FOOTBALL HEROES?

Check out heroesfootball.com
for quizzes, games, and competitions!

Plus join the Ultimate Football Heroes
Fan Club to score exclusive content and
be the first to hear about
new books and events.
heroesfootball.com/subscribe/